□~~

Prai:

MW01135656

and Memories that Live in the Bones

□~~~□~~~□

"*The Blue Box and Memories that Live in the Bones* is the type of book you want to curl up with in front of a crackling fire with a hot cup of coffee. Cozy, comforting, amusing, and brimming with heart, Mabry's prose absolutely shines. Though she doesn't shy away from hard things, her stories fill you with a warm glow and the desire to delve into your own anatomy for the memories that live there."
 −ANNA LEE HUBER, USA Today Bestselling Author of *A Fatal Illusion*

□~~~□~~~□

"Her great-aunt said, 'Memories live in the bones,' but Sharon Mabry extracts them with precision and deft expertise, sharing them on the pages of her memoir, *The Blue Box and Memories that Live in the Bones*. Poignant, with clever descriptions and sometimes laugh-out-loud humor, Mabry's personal stories transport us to our own similar childhood experiences; we are immensely grateful for that journey."
—JULIA BREWER DAILY, Award-winning author of *No Names to Be Given* and *The Fifth Daughter of Thorn Ranch*

□~~~□~~~□

"I had the pleasure to hear Sharon Mabry discuss her book, *The Postmaster's Daughter*, at the 2023 Writers Conference at Austin Peay State University in Clarksville, TN. I was impressed by her words and her delivery and recognized that she is an accomplished storyteller.
"This led me to read, *The Blue Box and Memories that Live in the Bones*, a general biography of her life, highlighted by eighteen specific stories. I appreciated the openness of the sharing of her biography, especially two stories. 'Living in Sin' is the story of her wedding and all the challenges that can accompany the event. In 'Retirement or Abandonment', Mabry shares her struggle to decide when and if to retire. Many readers of her personal stories will

recognize situations in their own lives. Also, this book will inspire other writers to share their own life experiences. It has me."
—Rick Gregory, author of *The Bell Witch in Myth and Memory: From Local Legend to International Folk Tale* (University of Tennessee Press, 2023).

□~~~□~~~□~~~□~~~□

The Blue Box
AND MEMORIES THAT
LIVE IN THE BONES

□~~~□~~~□~~~□~~~□

Sharon Mabry

To Susan,

Sharon Mabry

Thorncraft Publishing
Clarksville, Tennessee

First Edition, 2024

Published in the United States by Thorncraft Publishing.

This book, *The Blue Box and Memories that Live in the Bones*, is a memoir and reflects the author's recollections of her experiences over time. Some of the names, places, and events have been changed and/or compressed, and the dialogue has been recreated to the best of the author's memory.

Cover Design by Erica Trout Creative

Book Design by Shana Thornton

ISBN-13: 978-1-961609-03-7
ISBN-10: 1-961609-03-7

Library of Congress Control Number:
2023945172

Thorncraft Publishing
Clarksville, TN 37043
https://www.thorncraftpublishing.com

10 9 8 7 6 5 4 3 2 1

For my husband, George

Contents

☐~~~☐~~~☐~~~☐~~~☐

The Blue Box

AND MEMORIES THAT
LIVE IN THE BONES

□~~~□~~~□~~~□~~~□

Prologue

Where do memories live? Are they only in the hippocampus that's located in the brain's temporal lobe? Is that where I remember being six years old and running through the backyard after a small beagle dog named Spotty or a time when I got hiccups while singing in front of an auditorium full of people? I feel I'm there when I remember those events. Yes, it seems they are stored there with the individual details being located in the prefrontal cortex. Very scientific explanation, I guess. But there is more, much more.

What about body memory? It's defined as the sum of all of the body experiences we've had in the past, whether tactile, motor, pleasant, or painful, and the ability to sense what the body is doing at all times (proprioceptive) as well as the automatic things that go on in the body without having to think about them (interoceptive) and their accompanying emotions. So that's why I remember the feeling I had when I ate something I loved and might still crave, like chocolate-covered donuts that I no longer eat because they contain too much sugar for my diet. Just thinking about those donuts makes me shiver and want to drive across town to my favorite place where even from the parking lot the sugary donut smell makes your toes curl.

Then there is that dreaded emotional memory, some of it good and some of it bad. The scientists say that emotional events are processed in sensory systems and transmitted to the medial temporal lobe for the formation of an explicit memory about the emotional situation and then to the amygdala for the formation of an emotional memory. Super scientific! So, that's why I remember a feeling of dread and a tightness in the chest when recalling some experience that didn't go so well, like taking an algebra test in ninth grade and knowing that I didn't know what "x" meant, or why it meant something, and was certain I would fail the test even though I had been tutored every Wednesday night by my aunt who was the algebra teacher. It's also remembering the feeling of exhilaration when I heard that thunderous applause the first time I won an award for spelling in the fifth grade.

The brain is always editing, editing, editing. Memories that were once clear might start to fade or they may change a bit as time goes on. You might remember something five years from now that you don't remember now, when something happens to "jog" your memory and cause a shift in your perspective to reveal a detail you thought was long forgotten. As Nora Ephron famously wrote, "I remember nothing." But, in the end she remembered quite a lot. And most of us do. We just don't think about it very often until there's a reason to do so.

Some people seem to remember everything that ever happened to them and every person they ever met. I am not one of those people. I have a good friend who remembers every dress I wore for every concert that I sang when she attended and everything that I ever sang on that concert when, on occasion, I can't even remember singing the concert. Another friend seems to remember every person who came across his path during his life back to age three, telling numerous stories of people with such great detail that I've suggested he leave his brain to science for study to see what allows him to be the super memory gatherer that he is. In the end, it may be as my great Aunt Doshia used to say, "Your memories are in your bones."

There are plenty of memories and stories from my life that I recall as being hilarious, sentimental, carefree, and of course, quite sad. I've allowed several of them to coalesce and finally find a place in this collection for reflection on their sentiment, their revelations, and their humor. I have approached life with as much humor as possible, even when things did not appear to be humorous. It has brought a joy to life that might not have been there otherwise. I did not come from a family that had or displayed humor in their daily lives, so I don't know why I have it. Perhaps I was searching for the lightness that I feel when I laugh.

I grew up in a small town just at the foot of the Smoky Mountains in East Tennessee where the people pronounced my name more like "Sharn" than Sharon. There's not a diphthong in sight and I heard words like "sigogglin" from my mother anytime she saw something that was a little crooked or that leaned a little to one side, and the mashed potatoes we ate for supper would be called "arsh" potatoes by my father. They were his favorite.

I was born July 16, 1945, the day when the world's first nuclear explosion occurred. On that day a plutonium implosion device was tested at a site located 210 miles south of Los Alamos, New Mexico, on the plains of the Alamogordo Bombing Range, known as the

Jornada del Muerto. The code name for the test was "Trinity." But I was born in Newport, Tennessee on that day, and my mother's hair fell out, not because of the bomb blast but because she was allergic to the ether given to her as an anesthetic. When it grew back in it was mostly white. She couldn't dye it because she was allergic to the dye. So even as a young woman she had grey in her hair, a condition that made her self-conscious. She felt people would think she was older than she said and that was an unsettling thought, especially since my father was three years younger. Apparently, women were not supposed to be older than their husbands in those days. She spoke of it many times during her life and though her grey hair turned very white at the end, it was a beautiful kind of white, the kind that people want to have when they go grey. No need to dye hair like that. Unfortunately, I didn't inherit my mother's lovely white-grey naturally wavy hair. When my hair turned grey it was a yellow-grey, more like my father's hair, no waves in sight and a type that needs definite help of some kind.

I haven't lived in Newport full-time since going off to college in 1963, but I go back as often as I can. When I cross the plateau heading toward Knoxville and see the Smoky mountains in the distance with the shadowy purples and greys, constantly changing, and smell the tobacco barns and fried pies in the fall, I can exhale. The air feels and smells different. I feel lighter and more carefree. It is still home and a part of my bones and soul that will always be there, even when I am here no longer.

I don't remember much of my early years before we moved to town (Newport). We initially lived out in the county with my great Aunt and then in a house of our own across the road from hers for a year or so until I was five. I remember the houses we lived in and a few details that have become stories for me to tell, but not much more. Once we settled in Newport around 1950, things become clearer to me about my growing up years. This was the 1950s and early 60s and, in those days, the weather was not so hot, there was more snow in the winter and at an earlier time of the year. I lived only a couple of blocks from the grammar school in one direction and a couple of blocks from the high school in the other direction, so I walked to school every day from age six to age seventeen. I passed by the house of our doctor, my piano teacher, friends and friendly neighbors every day whether there was sun, rain, or snow. I knew everybody on those blocks and saw them regularly, could call them by name. They knew me and some would wave as I walked past their house, or their dog would come out to greet me and get a pat on the head on my way to school.

It was a perfect place to live, a welcoming place filled with people my parents knew on a first name basis. The neighborhood was shady with big trees and sidewalks that kept you safe from the passing cars. Music wafted from my piano teacher's house across the street from mine at all hours of the day and night. She not only taught piano, but violin, trumpet, accordion, and other instruments as well as voice. I started taking piano lessons at age six and voice at nine. So, I was at her house twice a week to soak up all of the knowledge she had to give until I went to college at eighteen. Once in a while, my lesson would be at 7:30 in the morning before school started at 8:30. I was never a morning person and even then, it was hard for me to get up and get ready for school on time let alone a piano lesson at 7:30. Sometimes her cook would bring in homemade biscuits and fried rabbit. I remember the first time she asked me if I would like some rabbit and a biscuit. I must have been about eight years old, and I had never eaten rabbit, but I took a bite of the fluffy biscuit with the sweet tasting rabbit in between the layers and said, "I like this. Could I have one to take to my mother? I don't think she's ever had one." She gave me one to take home, but my mother was not pleased that I had asked for another biscuit. I remember her calling Mrs. Hickey to apologize for my rudeness, but Mrs. Hickey said it was fine and continued to give me those delicious rabbit and biscuits whenever my lesson was early in the morning and occasionally gave me an extra one to take with me to school.

Back then, the springs were cool and the lemonade in the summer was so sweet and addictive that you craved sugar for at least two weeks. Of course, I was getting sugar from other sources since my mother was a fabulous cook in the Southern style and made mouth-watering desserts on a daily basis; chocolate cake with caramel icing, cobblers with fresh blueberries, strawberries, or peaches, a stack cake with seven layers of cookie dough with cooked spiced apples in-between, and my favorite thing in the world, chocolate cream pie with meringue so tall that it seemed to float on that luscious bed of chocolate. My father always wanted a coconut cake for his birthday, and he ate most of it over a three-day period since I hated coconut and mother seemed not to like much of it either.

Mother liked to do everything in the kitchen by herself, so I never learned to cook until I got married and had to make up for lost time. When I married, I asked her for some of her recipes, but I found that many of them contained steps like "stir until it looks right" or "don't let it boil too long" or "check to see if it's ready." After prodding, I did get some clearer, more specific, descriptions of what to do but nothing ever turned out quite the same as when she made it in her old pots—she declared that new pots would ruin everything, and she might have been right—with a long-ago habituated pattern in mind that couldn't be duplicated. When we had company, she would make three or four meats, usually a baked ham, a beef roast or swiss steak, smothered pork chops, and fried chicken. Creamed corn, fresh peas, baked beans, mashed potatoes, and green beans would be on the menu. There would be a congealed salad with fruit in it and a lettuce one with cucumbers. There was always cornbread with butter melting on the side, and dinner rolls or biscuits. Two or three desserts from her favorites would come out at the end. So, for many years after I left home, I enjoyed all of those foods on visits to her house and stopped trying to make them, choosing to go in another direction with my cooking, one that I could understand and had much less fat and sugar. Was mine better? Probably not. It was probably better for me but the memory of the food she cooked still lingers in my mind and I want a chocolate cream pie at every birthday, still.

The summers were cooler in those days. We didn't have air conditioning until I was about twelve when a den was added to the end of the two bedroom red-brick house on the hill and a window air conditioner suddenly appeared in that room to cool us off. We used fans everywhere else, one at the kitchen door, one in the hall between bedrooms, and one in the living room. But we really didn't need that air conditioner most of the time. We were used to the usually moderate heat with the slight breeze blowing from the mountains in the summer that didn't last past September when the days began to be cooler, and the nights brought sweaters out of the closet. Weather patterns have changed, and those days are gone.

Once the den was built, I stayed outside a lot on the attached covered back porch with my big furry dog, Mouton, and the duck. My parents had given me a baby duck for Easter back when people were doing such things and they assumed it would die, because apparently, most of them did die. I was about ten or eleven when they made that mistake. I guess it liked living with us and decided to trick them and live for many years as a companion to my dog and to me. I loved that duck. It followed me everywhere inside and outside the house. Was it male or female? We didn't know and no one seemed to know how to tell so we named it Donald. One day it surprised us and laid an egg, but we still called it Donald. Once my parents realized it wasn't going to die, they bought a small plastic wading pool for it to swim in. On some days, Donald and Mouton would both be in the pool splashing water everywhere. Donald thought she was a dog, I think, because she ate with Mouton and slept in the doghouse on the back porch with Mouton, sometimes her head on his back. They were best friends, and both lived long lives, even after I left the house for college.

My parents grew up on farms on opposite sides of the county and never knew each other until they were young adults and in the midst of World War II. They married in 1944, when my father was in the navy and stationed at Camp Perry, Virginia. My mother was a hairdresser during those early days and then a stay-at-home 'Mom' for most of her married life. I know very little of how they met or who their friends were during those times. Mother would sometimes mention a Mabel or Geraldine as being friends at Austin Peay Normal School, a two-year teacher-training school (which is what Austin Peay State University was called back in the early forties), but she had lost contact with them. I tried to help her find them years ago with no luck. I don't know who they were or what happened to them. She never talked much about her time at Austin Peay except to say that she remembered when all the boys left to go to war and never encouraged me to go there to college, so it is most ironic that I ended up being a professor of music there for fifty-two years. I have a picture of her in a family collage standing in front of Harned Hall, a building now used for offices and classes, but was once the dorm where she lived in 1941-42. She died in 2004 at the age of 82.

My father joined the navy when he was eighteen years old. He served one tour of duty without seeing any combat, returning home to work in a rayon plant and rising to a managerial position before he retired early at fifty-six, due to rheumatoid arthritis, a cruel disease that he would not survive, dying at age sixty-six in 1992. Throughout my life, my father was mostly silent when he was at home, so I never had a real conversation with him about anything except when he was stripping a piece of antique furniture and turning it into a beautiful object. He would show me what he was doing and explain how it would take layers of paint off the cherry wood that he was trying to reveal. I remember him laughing and enjoying himself when he was barbequing chicken or hamburgers in the summer and trying to keep Mouton from grabbing the chicken off the grill. He attended every piano and voice recital I gave over the years in Newport, even when Mother stopped coming because she said it made her too nervous. By the time I was in high school, I was a majorette with the high school band and twirling batons was on my resume. At one point, it was decided that we should twirl fire batons, which was all the rage. I still remember my father standing in the back yard with the hose pointed at me while I practiced with that fire baton so that if my hair caught on fire, he could put it out pretty fast, or so he thought. Fortunately, he never had to find out and that craze didn't last long. We gave it up from fear of disaster. Though he was always there when I needed something, he worked and lived his life outside my perspective.

My parents barely talked about their past and never talked about their life with each other. I never bothered to ask until they were much older, and they would just say something like, "Oh, it was hard back then." When I did ask much later in my life, and after my father died, my mother would say, "Well, young'un,' so many things happened to me that I don't want to remember." She would shake her head and that would end the conversation. I wish I had probed more, asked more pointed questions, seemed interested at a younger age. But we didn't talk about things that involved the two of them. Sometimes, Mother talked around the edges of her growing up years; her mother as being quite a disciplinarian and getting slapped for minor infractions and how she learned to cook from her mother. She had five siblings, some of whom still lived in Newport, but several had moved north during the war and communicated with her rarely. Others came to visit often. Mother didn't talk about her childhood and their years on the farm except to say, "They kept the place going as best they could during the depression." But there was never much detail, always keeping her feelings close to the chest, never exposing how she really felt about any of it, but I knew that there was plenty that could be discussed. When pressed there would be a telltale change in her face, a leaving the room when she didn't want to continue the conversation, or an abrupt change of subject.

Who was she back then? How was she different when I knew her or was she different then? Is it possible to live with parents for many years and not really know who they are? I think so. I was an only child, and I never really knew who they were.

The stories in this collection about my parents and my husband of fifty-six years are true, as I remember them, and from my perspective. Some are memories that still make me laugh a lot or wonder how it could have happened and others are tinged with regret. Some names have been changed for privacy reasons. They show us to be mostly normal but eccentric at times, though one of my relatives always says that we have a looney side to our family. I don't disagree! Some stories are meant to be humorous and some deal with serious issues that plagued my family and perhaps plague many other families. In the end, they are presented with love, humor, and contemplation.

Flower Power

"Don't you drive a Dodge?" Daddy said as he leaned over the bright orange and green flowered armchair crowded into the corner between the floor model TV and the door to the hall. Both hands were cupped around his eyes, trying to block out the glare of the den lights on the windowpane. It was ten o'clock at night, dark outside and though there was a streetlight on a pole at the end of the driveway, it was hard to see Mrs. Hickey's house across the road that ran between our place and hers.

A few minutes earlier, Daddy had risen slowly from his orange tweed upholstered rocking chair stationed next to the couch that matched the colorful armchair and walked casually over to the window, cocking his head as if trying to hear something outside. We all looked in his direction, but nobody asked what he was doing. He'd been standing there for a few minutes peering into the blackness while Mother talked to the slim, tuxedoed boy sitting up pole straight on the—as close as I can get to the door in case I need to run—end of the long couch and I was stationed at the other end.

There was enough room between us for three people to sit comfortably and Mother's large family had done so on many occasions when they came to visit for the Christmas holidays. Cousins, aunts, and uncles would pack into the knotty pine den and squeeze into every available space until the allotted time for the visit ended or a large meal was served in the dining room. This time there was no one to make the couch look smaller than it was, just this big cavern looming between us.

My prom date drummed the wooden arm of the couch in the silence between Mother's questions and I kept readjusting the scratchy crinolines under my dress hoping this inquisition would be over soon.

"Yes sir, it's my papa's car," Preston replied in an almost inaudible squeak while Daddy continued to stare out the window.

We'd made it back home with fifteen minutes to spare. It was my first date in a car, and we'd driven a whole block to the high school for the prom where we were chaperoned by what seemed like two adults for every student. My house was almost close enough for Mother and Daddy to watch the car's taillights turn into the school driveway.

I was in the ninth grade, had on a new, green, tea length dress with ribbons all down the back and shoes to match. They were a half size too small because Miller's department store in Knoxville didn't have my exact size. When I tried them on, I'd insisted they felt just fine after Mother said, "What a shame. Since they don't have your size, you'll just have to wear a pair that don't match the dress."

Now my toes were scrunched into joint-locked balls, and I wondered if I would ever be able to walk with flat feet again. After two self-conscious hours of standing around the punch bowl—trying to think of something to say to my date and his friends—and several uncoordinated attempts to dance with a moving target, I was now relieved to be sitting in the den in awkward silence while my parents quizzed Preston, this fair-haired high school junior who must have discovered cologne made with Listerine. They asked about everything that had happened since we left the house at 7:00.

We lived on a hill and the driveway had a steep slope with a level rise at the top where we parked our car. Visitors had to park on the slope behind our car since it was a one-car width driveway. Preston had never been to our house and since my parents had warned him not to park on the street in front, he had pulled up into the driveway as close to our car as he could get.

Parking on the slanting street down at the bottom of our yard was treacherous since cars came whizzing around the corner to the left of our house and regularly banged into anything that might be sitting on the side of the road just outside their view until it was too late to put on the brakes. People that lived in the neighborhood knew never to leave cars there, but sometimes out-of-towners or salesmen parked down there just before being hauled off by a wrecker. We could hear the crush of metal all the way into the back yard. One time, a big dump truck came flying around the corner and hit somebody's blue Valiant that had been left there when it ran out of gas. When Daddy came back to the house after walking down the street to see what happened, he said, "I reckon that sucker'll know better than to run out of gas on this hill again. They ain't two pieces in the same pile down there."

I hadn't really wanted to go to the prom with Preston. Since he was older, we had no classes together and had only spoken a few times at school. But when he asked, Mother said it would be rude to refuse since his mother was an old friend. Apparently, this was an arranged date. So, I responded with a doubtful "yes." The only other "dates" I'd had weren't really dates, not like this date. I'd walked downtown to the movies on Saturday with a group of friends—girls and boys—to see the latest show at the walk-in or go to a church social, but never been out alone with a boy by myself and never in a car.

"Did you put on your emergency brake, Preston?" Daddy said slowly while picking up his glasses off the top of the television and squinting out the window again. The TV was turned down low but began broadcasting a country music show that originated from Knoxville. The sudden onslaught of lively music momentarily interrupted Mother's barrage of questions. She hated country music 'til the day she died so she got up and turned the station asking, "Preston, what do you do in your spare time?" He seemed not to have an immediate answer and was fixated on Daddy's back, but eventually sputtered out something about floral arrangements.

"Well, I reckon that may come in handy, boy. Looks like your car is firmly planted down yonder in Mrs. Hickey's flowerbed. It must've rolled off the hill. I was afraid of that," Daddy drawled, shaking his head.

"I thought I heard something a few minutes ago and sure enough, down there it is. I can't tell from here if it missed her house or not. You've got to put on your emergency brake if you park on this hill," Daddy said, turning to look at Preston.

Preston jumped up from the couch and rushed to the window. When he turned back around, he looked paler than ever with eyes that seemed to be stuck in the wide-open position.

Mother, having gotten out of her chair to see for herself said, "Lordy, Lordy. I'd better go call your house and tell 'em what happened. Now you all go down there and see what kind of shape it's in."

She hurried down the long hall to the phone and Daddy and Preston went out the back door, around the house, and down the driveway while I watched from the window. Mrs. Hickey's outdoor lights had come on and I could see three people standing in the yard looking at the car wedged against the side of her house. They talked, gestured, and walked around the scene for about half an hour. Then Daddy and Preston came back up the driveway, got in Daddy's car and left. Preston never came back into the house.

When Daddy got home he walked into the den and said, "I bet he's gonna know where the emergency brake is from now on. That car's in some shape on the back end. I told his daddy they'd have to drag it outta there. I doubt it's drivable."

"Well, I'm glad you took him home, poor boy. His daddy was so mad he wouldn't come get him anyway. He was gonna make him walk home this late," said Mother.

"Naw, I didn't mind taking him home, but it's gonna take a week to get that Listerine smell out of my car."

I saw Preston a few days later from across the road. After his car had been towed by a wrecker, he spent the next three weeks every day after school and on Saturdays working in Mrs. Hickey's flower garden replanting flowers, replacing bushes, and repairing the ruts caused by the car when it slammed over the berm into her lovely side yard. I felt bad about how it all turned out.

That was the only time I wore those green shoes or the dress that birthed them. Preston and I avoided eye contact for the next two years until he graduated, and I never saw him again.

Several years later when I was planning my wedding, Mother said she thought the best place to have the flowers done was at The Flower Place downtown. I said that was fine. As we drove there to discuss the possibilities with one of the employees she said, "Do you remember the time Preston's car rolled off our hill into Mrs. Hickey's yard?"

I laughed and said, "I don't think he ever got over that. He could never look me in the face again. What ever happened to him?"

"Well, he got married right after graduation. Now he owns The Flower Place and has six kids, two sets of twins. Can you believe it?"

I was glad to hear he found somebody who liked Listerine.

A Way Out

"Well, I never," said my disapproving mother, as we tromped through a patch of tall grass and over a small ditch between our house and the handsome yellow brick one of our neighbors, the Delfin's—the only yellow brick house in town, according to Daddy. It sat on a small hill surrounded by huge shade trees and was approached from the road below by a long winding driveway that ended in a large parking area in front of the house. On that late, warm Sunday afternoon, my dog, Mouton, jumped over the ditch to greet us, wagging her tail and signaling she'd had a much better lunch than ours.

"Who cooks carrots with the tops on?" asked my father, as Mother admonished me with, "Keep walking. They'll think we're talking about them," when I turned around and looked back at the house. Since we were talking about them, I stared up at her and couldn't understand why that mattered. She took my arm, turned me back around and said, "Just get home and don't make a fuss." I hadn't actually said anything. I thought the carrots were fake, since you couldn't cut into them with a knife, so I hadn't tried to eat them. The carrots I'd had at home or school were always soft and smushy and barely needed chewing.

Once inside the house, Mother put her purse and hat on the dining room table and said, "Lordy, Lordy. Poor Marji. No wonder those kids are so thin."

"They don't look that thin to me," was met with a frown from Mother and an order to go to my bedroom and change out of my good clothes while she pulled out leftovers to heat up in case we were still hungry.

Hanging up his jacket in the hall closet, Daddy said, "Were we supposed to eat those tops? I never heard of that. They were just sprawled out all over the plate and mixed up with everything else." My father liked his food in sections on the plate and never let anything touch until it hit his stomach.

When the Delfin's had moved next door, Mr. Delfin came over to meet us and said they had just been married about a year and had moved from Chattanooga to run the family business. We'd never been invited to their house for a meal, though they'd lived next door to us for three or four years. Mr. Delfin, who my parents called "Lewin,"—but I was not allowed to—had come to the front door to talk to Daddy a few times and once to ask Mother if she could come over and show Marji how to wash clothes properly since she'd never done it before. He said their clothes needed attention.

When they first married, and the children came along, they'd had a maid who did all of the housework and took care of the laundry. For some reason, she no longer appeared at the house on a daily basis. Now, Marji was doing the laundry with little success. Apparently, Marji didn't know that certain kinds of materials had to be washed together and their clothes were getting "all gaumed up" with lint from towels and blankets and some things had shrunk to a shape that was unrecognizable, according to Mother. Another time, he came over to ask about joining one of the civic men's clubs in town. I'd heard that conversation, and the follow-up when Daddy told Mother they'd never let Lewin into the club because he was a Jew. She had agreed but when I asked why, she just said, "He won't fit in." Perhaps my father didn't fit in because he never became a member either.

"What took so long to get the food? Daddy asked. "We sat there staring at each other for an hour and a half before anything came out of the kitchen. I don't think she even scraped those carrots. They couldn't have been cooked more than three minutes and they were too big, hard as a rock and looked just plain dirty. I covered mine up with that gummy gravy, but I still couldn't eat 'em. Nasty stuff. What do you think was in that? It was like glue and that chicken was tasteless," said Daddy.

Mother said, "Well, you know Lewin said when they moved in that she'd never cooked until he married her. You'd think after five years, though, she'd have learned how to fix carrots, at least. I reckon she cooked that chicken without any salt and pepper and never put it in the oven to get it brown. It came out like boiled rubber. I bet that oven has never been used. At least you could eat the potatoes."

"Well, I'm starved. All I had was three bites of chicken, four sick-looking radishes, a few red potatoes that were barely cooked, and five rolls. At least those were store bought," said Daddy, sitting down to eat some leftover country-fried steak and creamed spinach from the night before.

"I felt bad because Lewin kept apologizing for the food and how bad it was. Marji's never going to be domestic, I'm afraid. She looked like she was going to cry. They need to get that woman back that cooked and cleaned for them. You remember those cinnamon buns she used to make?" said Mother, putting on her apron to start dinner.

"Yeah, they were pretty good. I wonder why they let her go?" said Daddy, reaching for another helping of beans.

Mr. Delfin owned a clothing store on Main Street just across from the train station in the middle of town. The large windows showed off the latest fashions in men's and women's clothing. Mother and I shopped the windows many times, but she said the clothes were too expensive for us, so we rarely went inside except to buy something really special, like a tie for Daddy to wear when he got promoted at work or a dress for me to wear on a piano recital. His was the only store in town that sold Capezio shoes, a handmade, fancy brand that fit skinny feet like mine. I had admired a pair of red ones and dreamed about having my very own pair, but I'd never tried a pair on until Mr. Delfin came to the house one day while I was putting away my schoolbooks in my room and told Mother, "We've acquired some new Capezio shoes that will work wonderfully with Sharon's new recital dress if you want to bring her down to try them on. Since you bought the dress at the store, I'll give you a discount on the shoes." He told her the price, but they were talking softly, and I didn't hear that part. Mother told him she would think about it. I knew those would be expensive shoes and we didn't have that kind of money to spend on shoes. So, I never mentioned it to her. But the next day when I came home from school, Mother said we were going down to Mr. Delfin's store to try on the Capezio shoes. I couldn't believe it and didn't expect that I would actually get them.

I sat on the chair with my right foot stuck out for Mr. Delfin to slip on the red butter leather shoe that fit like a glove. Then on went the left. I'd never felt anything that soft and knew that my feet would never be the same without them. I walked around, looked at them in the mirror, heard Mother say, "I appreciate this. Thank you," and watched as she pulled out one bill from her purse. I was in the sixth grade then and had grown to my adult height. My parents thought I was going to be a giant, but I never grew another inch. My shoe size didn't change for at least four years, and I wore those Capezios on special occasions until I was in high school. Years later, Mother told me that he sold her the shoes for $1 and told her it was because she was such a loyal customer. But she knew that it was because he had seen me walk to school on at least two occasions wearing shoes that were falling apart because we did not have the money to buy new ones when I needed them. Knowing this, he had offered shoes on long-term credit to her, but she had refused. This time, she accepted his kindness.

It was the 50s and Mr. Delfin always dressed up in a nice suit and drove a new Buick that was washed every week by one of his employees. He went to work early every morning and his wife stayed home with the children unless he took her out on Sunday afternoon in the car. We didn't know where they went but they would be gone for an hour or so. Eventually, Lewin told us he was teaching Marji to drive and that she would be taking a driver's test soon. We were surprised to hear that she had not passed the test when Lewin came over to borrow something a few weeks later. He said she still needed to figure out which was the brake and which was the gas. When the front door closed, Mother and Daddy had that look I was used to seeing which meant they would discuss it later and I would never know what they said.

A few weeks later, Daddy and Lewin were talking in the front yard while I was picking up dead sticks and I heard him say that Marji had failed the second and third test because she got too nervous and made mistakes. Her fourth try at the test ended in disaster when she backed into a fire hydrant while trying to parallel park and caused gushing water to flow all over the street. Lewin had been embarrassed and decided that it would be her final try at the test.

"She will never learn to drive. This is the last straw," he said.

For several years, my parents and the Delfin's had talked across hedges, yelled over dogs barking to see how things were going, and we all watched out the kitchen window as Mr. Delfin carried odd objects and huge bags of groceries into their house and heard plenty of reprimands to their constantly barking collie, named Ginger, who was imprisoned in a long, narrow space in their back yard with a gate. She wasn't allowed in the house nor out in the yard to run. Mouton was free to go with me everywhere, except indoors, and sometimes waddled down the street—dangling her right front paw that was split in two parts—to several neighbors' houses to have a snack. So, I worried why the Delfin's dog was not allowed to come over. Sometimes, I'd go to the edge of my yard and talk to her so that she would feel like somebody knew she was there.

I had only heard her voice crying for help and wondered why she was never let out until one day in the late afternoon when someone must have left their gate open. Chaos suddenly erupted on our back porch as she lurched through the yard, chasing my duck, Donald—the one who turned out to be a girl after laying an egg—upending the plastic wading pool and spilling all of the duck's water onto the ground, and upside-downed the grill that Daddy had prepared with charcoal for a chicken dinner that evening. Soon after that, we heard her voice no more. They had given her away to a family out in the country. I pictured her running wildly for the first time, enjoying dreamed-about freedom from confinement.

Though invited, Marji had never been inside our house. We'd only talked to her a few times across the ditch or waved at her if she was walking out to take the trash to the bin. One day, she came all the way to the edge of her yard and just over the ditch between our houses but avoided looking at us much as she talked. She looked like she'd been crying. She told us that Lewin was several years older than she and that they met through a friend of her mother who was trying to find a husband for her. After all, "I was nearly twenty-five when we married and that is old where I come from." She never said where "come from" was but we guessed it was a long way from where she was now. She'd left her friends there and hadn't been able to find new ones.

Lewin told us she was a recluse. It took a dictionary to figure out what that meant since Mother's explanation was that she was "strange." I had a lot of relatives that Mother called "strange," which for them indicated a stint in jail, they drank too much, cursed a lot, had fights and broke a lot of nice dishes, or were just plain nuts. I didn't know Marji well enough to know if she was strange like my relatives or like Mr. Ed, a talking horse who starred in a TV show I watched every week.

Mother and Daddy had given me a huge, heavy, hard-to-pick-up dictionary that sat on the shelf in the den. I got it out and read the definition of "recluse" several times and decided Mr. Delfin was right. Marji seemed never to come out of the house or go anywhere since she didn't drive and wouldn't look at you when she talked. On the afternoon of our lunch at their house, I got it out again, read the definition of "strange" and decided that she was both a recluse and strange. We'd never met anyone like her and might not again, which made her even more intriguing.

They had two children, Mary and Joshua. I was about eleven or twelve years old on the lunch day. Mary was about five and her little brother was a toddler. They were not allowed to come over to play but that was okay since I was an only child, a good bit older, and spent most of my time practicing piano or reading books.

One day, when I was in the ninth grade and still wearing his Capezios, Mr. Delfin came to tell us that he was selling his store and his house, and they were moving to Chattanooga where his family lived. He explained that it was due to family obligations and that he would miss us and Newport. There had been rumors that his store had not been doing well for several years, that he had been too generous with customers in reducing prices, giving away merchandise, and not making ends meet. But Daddy said that he thought they had just had enough of Newport and had never fit in.

They drove off and we never saw them again. Marji never said "Goodbye." We spoke of them occasionally and wondered what happened to them. One day, years later, just after I married, Mother called to give me her weekly news. She said, "a friend of mine told me that the Delfin's children have done real well down in Chattanooga, but Lewin and Marji got a divorce. Can you believe that?"

Apparently, Marji had moved back to Philadelphia where she grew up. I guess she finally learned to drive.

Allergic to Life

"Yowza," said my doctor, as he leaned back in his chair, ran stubby fingers through thick black hair and stared at my right leg which had just been revealed from beneath my pants leg. The huge, red, angry splotches were mostly on the shin and right side and didn't go up very far but compelled a gape. Lifting the other pant leg, I said, "I think this one looks worse." He leaned in and agreed. After a few minutes of analysis, head scratching, peering through a magnifying glass at the leprosy-looking wannabees and asking questions about everything I'd done in the past month, he said, "I guess you're allergic to something. I'll give you a prescription for a steroid cream that will clear it right up." Having had previous relationships with steroid creams, I was skeptical and thought my doctor should know better since he'd been seeing me for about eight years and knew my history of allergic reactions, but I filled the prescription anyway.

My intuition was correct. After using the cream for two days, the splotches were redder, had grown like a teenage boy going through puberty, and now itched twenty-four hours a day. I was allergic to the cream. So, I threw it out and consulted my usual experts, the internet and two nature-based health magazines, and found that putting cold cloths—that had been soaked in baking soda—on the spots a couple of times a day would stop the itch and reduce the redness. It was a tedious endeavor that required carrying around small bags of baking soda on several out-of-town trips and took a couple of months to get rid of the spots altogether. But it worked. However, I still didn't know what had caused the outbreak of this menace, so I started to do some investigating and finally decided it was the socks and pants material I was wearing in the winter that had caused the eruption. Avoidance seemed to be the key. No more wool!

I come by my affinity for allergic reactions naturally. I grew up hearing that story of why my mother already had white hair in her late twenties. She said the doctor had given her ether when I was born, she was allergic to it, all of her hair fell out, and when it came back in, it was solid white and not the beautiful brunette I see in the old pictures of her when she was in college.

My earliest remembrance of Mother's allergy issues was when I was about eight years old. One afternoon, I was practicing piano in the living room while she was in the kitchen. I heard a loud thump. She had fainted and was on the floor. I called for my father who ran to the kitchen from the den, picked her up, put her on the couch, and told me to call Dr. Schultz, our family doctor, who lived just down the street. He answered the phone immediately and said he'd be right up. I remember standing in the hallway, watching and listening as he examined her, got her awake, and shaking his head, said to my father, "She's had an allergic reaction to the sulfa drug I gave her for bronchitis. I think she'll be fine, but she can't have any more of that drug." She'd had bronchitis for a few weeks, had stayed inside the house at the doctor's suggestion, and this was the third drug he'd tried to get rid of it. She'd apparently had an allergic reaction to all of them. As he walked to the door, he said, "Mrs. Cody, don't bother to stay in the house anymore. Just get on out and we'll stop taking anything right now and see how it goes. You seem to be allergic to everything." She did that and lived another fifty years. As far as I know, she never took another pill of any kind, not even aspirin, until she was admitted to the hospital a couple of years before she died and every drug they gave her then seemed to make her worse.

His words stayed with me when I discovered in my thirties that I was also allergic to two sulfa drugs, and four different antibiotics, given by two different doctors for different problems. The rashes and debilitation brought on by those incidents were immediate and self-defining.

I was the kid who never got vaccinated for anything because Dr. Schultz thought I might be allergic to the shots. I remember when he gave me a penicillin shot for something and everything went dark. I was about ten years old, and my mother was in the room when I had the bad reaction. I awoke to hear him say, "I guess she's inherited your allergies to drugs. Heaven help us." So, when all of the children lined up in the hall at school to get their polio vaccines in the 50s, I had a note saying I shouldn't get it and I never did. No one spoke of it, so I have no idea whether the students who had to get the shots envied me or wondered if I was an alien.

Mother's allergies were of all kinds. She couldn't wear or smell any perfume without her eyes turning red and getting wheezy breathing. She wore no makeup because of blotches that appeared on her face and could wash her clothes only in Tide and baking soda to avoid itchy skin and rashes.

My body seems to hate drugs of all kinds, but especially antibiotics. The list is long of the ones I've tried and know I can't take. They've caused rashes, welts, nausea, delirium, and digestive upsets that were life-threatening. Thus, after I had shingles a few years ago, I asked my doctor if I should get the shingles shot to prevent another attack and he said, "Well, you might be better off to just take your chances. You might grow two heads if you get the shot. Better safe than sorry." So, no shingles shot yet.

Some of my allergic reactions have caused laughter rather than concern. On two occasions, I looked like a raccoon with dark red, puffy circles around my eyes, once from small eye pad cleansers given to me by my ophthalmologist, who declared that I was the first person he'd ever known to be allergic to them, and another time after working in the plants on my deck without gloves. Apparently, I had touched my eyes before I washed my hands. I never let that happen again.

It's difficult to find a doctor who doesn't despair of patients like me and my mother. We don't react well to their suggestions and require a lot of searching for ways to treat issues without just writing a prescription that most people would find helpful or at least not react to in a horrible way. So, finding the right doctor and breaking them in, so to speak, has been a life's work. I've had some great ones with patience and caring, but I know that I've almost sent them over the edge several times with my strange illnesses and bizarre allergic reactions.

Once when my beloved doctor of many years discovered that I had developed chronic fatigue syndrome due to an overexposure to mold in the building where I worked, he suggested that I get a B-12 shot until I told him the story of my mother's reaction to a B-12 shot that caused her lips and eyes to swell shut and made her unable to breathe. Just as his nurse entered the room with the shot, he turned and said, "We're not going to do that," and sent her away. He turned to me, patted my hand and continued, "I think you should just start taking magnesium and B-12 sublingual in large doses." He was unlike the doctor I saw at another time who looked at my chart and said, "Nobody's allergic to Ringer's lactate," even though it had paralyzed me for several hours and nearly killed me during a hospital stay. He smirked as if I was completely nuts, took the notice out of my file, and threw it in the trash. I never went to see him again.

My latest adventure with allergic reactions came following cataract surgery when I had to use steroid eye drops for two months during that process. I had no issues while I was using the drug so never gave a thought to allergic reactions. However, a month or so after that I began to feel sick, my tongue turned green—a color that has always been one of my best but not for my tongue. I lost all ability to taste food and over a three-month period lost seventeen pounds and two clothes sizes. My doctor ordered many tests which all came back normal. He sent me to two specialists who could find nothing, but I still felt horrible and hated food, which was an anomaly for me since I have spent my life planning vacations around restaurants that I want to experience.

During this process, I was given yet another antibiotic by one of the specialists to kill some perceived bacteria that might be lurking in my gut. Predictably, I had a bad reaction to the antibiotic and almost ended up in the emergency room and had to stop taking it after two days. My husband had become concerned when I began babbling, looked extremely pale, and could no longer walk upright.

The final guru I met for this problem—whom I had been trying to see for three months—sat with me for several minutes, asked questions, read over my file, looked me over, declared that I was basically a very healthy specimen, and told me to stop taking anything, including the supplements I had been taking for years, to just get outside and go about my business and it would probably go away. I did, and it did! He had no idea what had caused my issue and had no other suggestion except to file an exorbitant bill which, fortunately, my insurance paid. My original doctor now believes that I was allergic to the steroid eye drops that I took for two months before, during and after the cataract surgery ordeal. He surmised that they had upset my digestive system in the most disagreeable way and caused chaos throughout my body.

As my pharmacist—who is quite familiar with all of my drug allergies—said, after finding out that I had a bad reaction to that antibiotic given by the specialist, "You always seem to get the weirdest things and there's just nothing you can take for them." Her assessment seems to be right on track.

At my most recent physical, my doctor, who has a great sense of humor, declared me fit and ended my visit with, "Try to stay away from antibiotics and doctors if at all possible and just go out and enjoy life." Sounds like good advice. I think Dr. Shultz has been reincarnated.

Living in Sin

"Her Mother and I do."

Daddy had practiced saying those five words while shaving, walking to his rusted-out Civic that had its paint eaten off by smokestack fumes at the plant where he worked, and at the end of his cigarette—the one he smoked after dinner since he worked his way down from two packs of Camels a day and Mother banished him to the back porch to keep smoke out of the house, though she still complained that washing his smoke-smelly clothes would kill her and that would surely happen before the wedding.

Narcissism had overcome me long before the wedding. I gave little thought to anything but sending out invitations, finding a wedding dress that worked with my freckles, picking out seven bridesmaids dresses and tuxes for the groomsmen, attending bridal showers, and finding a place for the rehearsal dinner since my in-laws were from out of town and had no idea where to hold it.

For weeks, every day was filled with plans of some sort—going to a farm out in the county to talk to a hog-calling, wild-haired woman my mother knew who, according to a friend of hers makes a good wedding cake; arranging for the florist and photographer; finding motel rooms for guests from Chattanooga, Florida, and New Jersey; and writing thank you notes for gifts that kept pouring in from the four-hundred or so invitations we had sent to my soon-to-be Father's Day afternoon wedding, June 18, 1967, at the First Baptist church in my hometown.

I had grown up in that church and sung solos there on a regular basis since I was eight years old. So, Mother thought that if anyone was left out of the invitation pool we would surely be banished from Heaven to some place where an air conditioning salesman would become rich quick. Once we had written down the names of every church member who ever crossed our path, the list was long. But we soon realized that some of our neighbors, several relatives who lived in places I had never heard of and certainly never visited and were known only to my mother, and a few friends from high school who I hadn't seen in four years and never really liked but were in choir or band with me, didn't go to that church but should be invited. So, the list grew almost overnight to about four hundred and fifty names.

Before they were all sent out, a few were purged due to some slight that Mother remembered from her high school days, a PTA meeting squabble, an odd interaction in the grocery store, or the fact that we weren't invited when their third cousin got married. Slash! Down to about four hundred.

Gifts appeared almost daily from the jewelry store where I had registered china and crystal patterns and from local department stores that dispensed toasters, towels in colors that were not on any color wheel I had ever seen and ashtrays with bears stuck on the sides. The house took on the look of a huge display case where everything was put in categories and placed on tables, stools, and chairs with the gift cards alongside so that anyone coming to visit could look at everything and know who sent it. This was tradition, according to Mother. She was apparently right, because aunts, cousins, and neighbors who had not been to visit in years showed up without much notice to see what loot had been acquired and who might have paid how much for which gift.

As activity picked up, tempers flared, decisions had to be made quickly, and absolutely no one seemed to be having a good time planning this event that would bring two families—with nothing in common—together for a few days culminating in a ceremony before a huge crowd of well-wishers with names that most of us couldn't remember or never knew.

At one point, Mother decided that she just wouldn't go to the wedding since I didn't like the dress she had picked out to wear. All I said was, "That's a color you've never worn before," which set off her declaration that I hated her and didn't want her to come, which was answered with, "Ok, if you don't want to come, just don't come." She stalked toward the kitchen, and I slammed the bedroom door.

Daddy was left alone in the hall and yelled, "Well, if you're not going then I don't have to wear that tight tux." But later that day I heard him in his bedroom in front of the mirror mumbling, "Her Mother and I do."

The bridesmaids were high school friends, college friends, the sister of the groom, and two cousins, seven in all, some I hadn't seen in quite a while. Several were coming in from long distances, as far away as Miami. I had picked out the avocado green sheer, flowing dresses with short trains because I like green and look good in green, not because any of them would look wonderful in green, especially that shade. The dresses were the shade of my mother's kitchen appliances, which was definitely "in." Remember, it was 1967.

After all, it was MY wedding.

There was no way all the bridesmaids could come to try on dresses, living in such disparate spots, so they sent their sizes, and the dresses were ordered. The dresses were to be mailed to each girl well in advance so that any needed alterations could be done before the wedding.

That plan sounded workable and there were no red flags until the day of the wedding when the matron of honor appeared in her supposedly floor-length dress that had been hemmed to a length suitable for salsa dancing. The flowing train, meant to just touch the floor in the back, was long enough to drag a good three feet behind her.

A larger problem surfaced when one of the bridesmaids arrived an hour before the wedding—she had not been able to come to the rehearsal dinner—stating that she had never tried on the dress because it had just arrived two days before and she assumed it would fit. Unfortunately, she was either much thinner or more optimistic than realistic when she gave the size for the order. The two-inch gap now causing the zipper to never meet its match had to be secured in some way. Fortunately, the flowing train would hide the zipper. Since no amount of pulling and tugging wedged her into it, we had to find something that would hold it in place until her last step down the aisle. I noticed one of the long white church napkins used for breaking bread lying on a table in the corner. I grabbed it and with one of the other bridesmaids—who happened to carry a needle and thread with her everywhere—sewed her into the dress twenty minutes before the wedding was to begin.

My mother-in-law dropped by the choir room where the wedding party had gathered as I was checking off the list of things that had to be done, a vision that solidified my approval rating in her mind for the rest of her life. She had discovered a kindred Type-A personality and knew that when it is announced that an asteroid is actually going to hit our planet, I will be making sure the plants have been watered and the towels have been folded right up to the end. We got along famously!

The preacher at the First Baptist Church was a handsome man in his early fifties, beautifully dressed at all times, and prided himself in delivering his sermons without notes. At the dress rehearsal the night before the wedding, everything went as scheduled. There were no issues to iron out and the preacher calmed any nerves by boasting that he had an impeccable memory and had presided over dozens of weddings without a single mistake.

I've often thought that my wedding was not really for me. I never saw the sanctuary fill with guests who probably exclaimed over the bouquets of flowers and beautiful candles. I never saw the flowing bridesmaids' dresses as they walked down the aisle to admiring eyes. I never heard the singer, nor the organist perform carefully chosen music prior to the service. I was getting dressed, sewing up zippers, and checking off lists during all of that.

I felt more like wedding planner than bride as I waited in the foyer with my bridesmaids and father, who looked like a most handsome betuxed lookalike of an infamous politician of the time. When the Wedding March started, we strode down the aisle, as practiced, and up to the front to meet the rest of my life. But, when we reached the front of the sanctuary, the process we rehearsed the night before suddenly changed. The preacher took my hands from my father and led me further up the steps onto the platform near the altar, leaving my father standing by himself at the bottom. I was confused. A whole section had been left out.

As I turned sideways to face my groom, I saw Daddy haltingly move toward his seat on the second pew with Mother. The preacher's memory had apparently failed for the first time in his life, and he had not asked, "Who gives this Bride in Holy Matrimony?" There never was a place to say, "Her Mother and I do." He never apologized nor seemed aware that he had totally changed the ceremony. Daddy told me later that he was glad he didn't have to say it, but I had already noticed that he looked sad when he sat on that pew.

At the wedding reception, several friends and relatives of the groom stuffed money into his hand or pocket saying, "Enjoy a steak dinner on me," something we planned to do on our honeymoon at Thunderbird Mountain Lodge in North Carolina, a couple of hours away. What a godsend! We had very little money of our own and not yet begun our summer jobs. We suddenly felt rich, at least rich enough to enjoy a few days of limbo without having to worry about where the next dollar would be found.

We waved goodbye to our parents and the wedding party and escaped to the mountains stopping at a roadside restaurant halfway between Newport and our destination. Since I had been in wedding mode all day and not eaten breakfast or lunch, I was starving. So, some of those pocket-crushed dollars came out to pay for steaks, french fries, and salad, plus a jumbo-sized chocolate dessert with ice cream for both of us. We ate it all with gusto.

The drive to the lodge took us around winding mountain roads that made for slow driving, but we finally arrived around 9:30 p.m. at the end of a hectic day full of surprises, joys, calamities, anger, good food, and expectation. We couldn't believe we were actually married after dating for three and a half years and were finally alone with no one to tell us what we needed to do next. But we had a good idea what that might be.

I had purchased four new nightgowns just for this occasion and was eager to see what kind of response each might elicit. So, I went into the bathroom to get dressed for bed but almost immediately started feeling a bit queasy. A bit turned into a lot and the need to get rid of everything I had eaten was overwhelming. So, I stayed in the bathroom for what seemed like an eternity, hoping it would subside. Every time I put my hand on the doorknob to leave it would get worse. I just froze in place waiting to see what was going to happen and afraid that I wouldn't make it back fast enough if I opened the door and left for even a second. After several minutes, my husband began to worry that I had climbed out the window and was already halfway down the mountain. He asked timidly through the door, "Are you alright in there?"

"I'm just having a little sick feeling. I'll be out in a minute," I said, trying to sound perky but knowing that I might not be out in a minute. They say that one forgets pain after a time, but I still recall that as being one of the worst stomachaches of my life. I could have saved my lingerie money and worn a sack that evening because most of it was spent in the bathroom with my husband pacing outside the door wondering if he needed to call an ambulance. Some people may be able to binge at night after a grueling day of nerve-wracking crises that include starvation but I'm certain that my genes come from the stock of those who never would have made it across the Great Plains in a covered wagon.

Several months later—after we had spent the summer working in a summer stock theatre, moved to Nashville for graduate school and a teaching job, and being at the height of the Vietnam War my husband had been drafted and rejected from the army three times for having high blood pressure—we received a letter from the State of Tennessee saying that we were not legally married because the minister who married us had never sent in a signed copy of an official document required by the state certifying that he was qualified to perform the ceremony.

Stunned and shocked does not quite cover it. It took some time to track him down since he had left our First Baptist Church for one in another city. But finally, it became official.

I wondered if he was still telling every bridal party that he had an impeccable memory.

Afterlife

"I've got to get this thing back to the antique mall before it closes," I said with purse in hand, holding open the front door for my husband who was hefting the bulky oak and leather strapped trunk down the stairs from the second-floor guest bedroom, where it had been staring into the hallway for the past two days. He grumbled under the load across the porch and out to my car. Something akin to calm came over my body for the first time since I had brought this relic into our house.

The bespectacled, spiky haired woman who sold it to me at the antique mall on Riverside Drive said it came from an old house out in the county and had belonged to someone who fought and died in the Civil War. She elaborated on the trunk's travels from place to place over the years, how it once contained letters from the fallen soldier, and how his one surviving relative had sold the house and emptied it of all contents at an auction. It was a fascinating story, and the trunk was perfect for the location I had in mind—the foot of the guest room bed.

I had been looking for an antique trunk like it for several years and couldn't believe my luck when I stumbled onto this one and managed to talk the proprietor down from $250 to $200. One of her workers who carried it to my car said, "You really got some history here. There's no telling what this old thing's seen." I learned later it was an omen better listened to than ignored. That was on a Saturday.

I drove home from the antique mall with the trunk in my back seat and for some reason kept feeling the need to look at it in the rearview mirror, as if it might be gone, have moved to the other side of the seat, or was trying to say something to me. But there it sat, just as it was placed by the worker until I arrived—broadcasting my find—to the surprise of my husband who never felt the need for anything to be placed at the foot of that bed. However, once in place, we agreed that it looked perfect there. It could be seen in two directions, straight ahead from the hall leading into the bedroom and when coming up the stairs from the first floor. I took it in from all sides in the room, the approach from the hall and while climbing the stairs. It presented no errors in judgment for having bought it. But for some reason, I began to feel uneasy and out-of-sorts the more I looked at it. I went back downstairs and tried to get the feeling out of my mind but felt compelled to go back upstairs several times that night to check on it, to see if it looked the same. The last time I dared approach it, I just peeked up the stairs from the bottom floor right before going to bed, but my sleep was elusive and edgy.

On Sunday morning, I awoke to find that the toilet in our master bath would not work. It was as if the whole mechanism inside the tank had been disconnected. It wasn't stopped up, just non-functioning. Thankfully, we had another bathroom upstairs and a half bath next to the dining room. So, we could wait until Monday morning to call the plumber. During the first half of the day, we used those two baths until my husband's voice rang out from upstairs just before dinner.

"You're not going to believe this, but now this toilet won't work either. It's just sitting here. I've tried everything, and it won't flush."
 I started to feel more nervous than I had before, as if it was hard to take a deep breath. I had a premonition that whatever was in that trunk was starting to pervade the entire house and take over our lives but tried to mark that up to watching too many scary movies over the years.

I hadn't said anything to my husband about this growing feeling that something sinister had entered our house. I remembered how he scoffed when my mother swore that for several days after her father died in 1976, she smelled a lit cigar coming from his bedroom every afternoon, something that was part of his persona, and one night caught a glimpse of him walking down the hall from his room to the den where he always held court. After a few days of these manifestations, everything returned to normal, and she never talked of ghosts again until 1992, when my father died. Prior to his death, he had been ill for many months and had slept in the guest bedroom while she slept in the bedroom just down the hall. Once again, she called me to say that she heard Daddy's ghost getting up in the middle of the night and moving the creaky bathroom door that connected to his room. She locked her bedroom door thinking it would keep him out of her room, but she couldn't sleep. This went on for three nights until she finally went into his bedroom on the fourth night before going to bed and said, "You have to quit this and go away. I'm too scared. Just stop it." She never heard anything again but started sleeping in the den on the couch or in her lounge chair and continued doing that until she went to an assisted living almost ten years later. Her bedroom became a place for storage and the bed was left unused.

I never doubted Mother in her assertions because I remembered experiencing the attempt to reclaim my aunt and uncle's house in 1963 by the ghost of its former owner. They had lived next door for several years and made friends with the owner who lived alone and had eventually bought the house from her with the agreement that she could stay upstairs in the bedroom attic apartment as long as she lived. She lasted about a year.

My parents and I had taken yearly trips up north to visit some of my eccentric Mother's relatives since I was a young child. But, it had been a couple of years since our last visit. We always stayed with this particular aunt and uncle, but this was our first visit to their new location, a lovely, early twentieth century home with gardens and a koi pond with walkways around it. It happened that this visit occurred during the holidays while I was home from college and just following the assassination of President John F. Kennedy. We were to be there four nights.

We had no idea until after we arrived that there had been unusual, inexplicable happenings at the house that had required hiring a private detective to see if someone was trying to scare them. That information came out only in the last few minutes of our stay.

Upon arrival, we happily greeted everyone, put away our luggage, were shown around the house and garden, had a snack, and found our seats in the living room to watch the funeral of President Kennedy on the black and white TV. We sat in stunned silence for several minutes watching the sad processional when the TV suddenly turned off. In 1963, a TV was turned on and off with a knob that sounded an audible click, or at least this one and the one we had at home were of that kind. We all heard the click. How was that possible?

"What happened?" asked Mother, sitting up on the edge of the couch. It was obvious that the electricity didn't go off because the lights were still on. "Oh, it's been doing that a lot lately," said my aunt. "We've got to get somebody out here to see what's causing that," my uncle said, getting up to turn the TV back on. Click. We continued watching and nothing more was said about it until after dinner when I heard my parents whispering about it in the bathroom next to our bedroom.

Apparently, Mother was a little nervous about that TV incident and the fact that the previous owner's fifteen-year-old parrot named Charlie had died for no apparent reason just a few days before. The bird had a vocabulary of more than thirty words and was an incessant talker but had stopped altogether after the owner died. Over washing dishes, my aunt had related all the details of its demise and told Mother that the owner kept the bird in a cage in the dining room. I noticed the covered cage in the corner when we took the house tour. They had taken care of the bird after the old lady's death, feeding it a special diet, keeping regular vet visits until one day when they awoke to find it dead at the bottom of the cage. They put its body in a little box and took it to the vet who had taken care of the bird for years. He expressed shock to see such a young, healthy bird lifeless on his table and said he could find no reason why it died. His guess was that it had been so attached to the owner that it died of a broken heart.

"Charlie had been with her since he was a baby, sitting on her shoulder to watch TV and calling out to her from its cage when it needed to talk or get out for a while to roam around the house," said the vet who had appeared to have tears in his eyes, causing my aunt to feel even more guilt than she already had prior to this visit.

We went to bed that night around 9:00. The house was quite dark, except for one hall lamp that sat on a little antique smoker outside the bathroom. My parents were in the front bedroom, and I slept with my cousin in the bedroom on the other side of the hall. Around 2:00 a.m. I woke up to hear low voices coming from my parents' bedroom. I crept out of bed and opened the door to see light coming from their room. Just as I stepped into the hall to go to the bathroom, the lights came on in the bedroom I had just left. I turned around to see my cousin still asleep in the bed but the light switch by the door was turned up. I had not touched it.

The door to my parents' bedroom creaked open and my father whispered, "Who turned on all the lights?"

"I don't know," I said, crossing the hall to their room. "The light in my bedroom just came on by itself as I got up to see what was going on." As I finished my last few words, the lights started coming on one at a time in every room on the bottom floor, living, dining, kitchen, bathroom, and hallways. We stood in the hall and stared at each other watching it happen. It reminded me of a grade B movie I had seen the year before where the lights kept coming on in strange places and at strange times. Unfortunately, everyone was swallowed up by a large dark hole at the end. Great movie!

Just about that time, my aunt came down the stairs in her Christmas tree robe with giant curlers in her hair. "I'm so sorry about this. There's something wrong with the electricity in this house. I should have told you. The lights have been coming on and going off by themselves for a while now. We called an electrician just two days ago and he says there's nothing wrong, so we've tried to live with it. But there's got to be a short circuit somewhere."

"Well, it'll get your attention in the middle of the night," Daddy said as he went back into his bedroom. Mother had come out looking worried. "You don't think the house could catch on fire, do you?" she said, wrapping her robe around her shoulders.

"No, no, that electrician says the fuse boxes and wires are in great shape, not to worry about something like that. Besides, you all are at the front of the house so if you need to get out, it's pretty easy. Just open your bedroom door and bolt right out that front door."

We went around the house and turned off all of the lights and went back to bed in our respective bedrooms. But I didn't sleep at all, waiting for the lights to come back on.

The next morning, my uncle came into the kitchen from downstairs where he had been in the basement that was filled with the old woman's excess furniture: a beautiful cherry wood antique dining table and eight chairs, a few side tables, and three overstuffed chairs that once were in the living room. We were shown this part of the house during the tour. My aunt and uncle had bought some new furniture and moved these pieces downstairs when she died.

"I thought I heard those chairs move again last night," he said as he sat down to his eggs and biscuits. "I had to put them all back around the table, as usual." Silence.

We spent that day away from the house visiting other relatives in the area, having one-of-a-kind hand-tossed pizza, and trying to figure out what was going on at that house. I had already decided it was the previous owner's ghost trying to get rid of all of us and had my bag packed and ready to go in case she got in bed with me that night.

The second evening went without incident until we all went to bed. I was still awake when I heard the chairs move one at a time under the room where I slept. I counted eight. The lights came on again one at a time throughout the entire house and just as I got up to go into the hall, they started going off again one at a time. This time, no one got up to see what was going on.

At seven o'clock the next morning, Mother knocked on my door and said, "Get dressed, we're going home." By eight we were in our car, not having had breakfast, headed toward a little diner down the road. That was my last trip up East to visit relatives. My parents went back one more time, I think, but they stayed at a motel near the diner where we ate on our way out of "The Twilight Zone."

"I know you'll think I'm crazy like my mother, but I have to get rid of that trunk upstairs," I said to my husband, getting into bed. I could no longer go up the stairs without feeling like I needed to run. As predicted, he was not having that explanation, so I dropped it until just before breakfast on Monday morning when we discovered that the toilet in the half bath would no longer work.

"It has to go now," I said, with emphasis, and called the antique mall lady to let her know it missed her and was coming back.

"I can't believe you're just going to take this thing back without getting a refund," my husband said, slamming the door to the back seat of the car.

"When I called her, she said they don't give refunds, but she'd put it back on the floor and let me know if it sells and I can come back and pick up the money, minus her commission. Maybe I'll get back some of the money. We'll see."

"Two hundred dollars down the drain," he mumbled.

I grabbed my purse, jumped into the car, rolled down the window, and said, "Well, which would you rather have, two hundred dollars or a haunted trunk and no toilets that work?" I wanted that thing out of my car before it got infected, too. At this point, I didn't care whether I got the money back or not.

My car practically flew back to the antique mall, the trunk was unloaded, and I began to breathe in a normal rhythm. While I was gone, the plumber was called to come to the house later that afternoon, but within the hour and one by one, all three toilets began working again with no sign of anything ever having been wrong. So, he was called again and told not to come.

Two weeks later the trunk was sold, and I got all of the money back but wondered whose life was being taken over now.

Fly By Night

Mother and I stared out the den window as the termite slayer-man, backed down the steep driveway onto the winding road in front of the house. All six hairy, collarless, unvaccinated, non-spayed or neutered dogs barked after his get-away. Horns started blowing when he bumped out in front of a car that came whizzing around the telephone pole sitting at the edge of the sharp corner on the right and a motorcycle that lurched out of nowhere from the sloping hill on the left. Tires squealed and somebody yelled, "Move it," as he slammed on the brakes and barely missed the neighbor's parked car. Mother frowned, turned away from the window, walked toward the long hall into the kitchen, and announced, "He won't get a dime outta me. If he calls back, I'm gonna tell him we already got somebody else to kill those flying ants. This house never has had termites and never will. Don't you pay him a cent. And if I hear that you talked to him again, I'll change my will. You hear me?"

What will? I'd been trying to get her to make one for years. He threw up his hands and rolled into the middle of the road, halting traffic in both directions. I left him there, glanced down the hall, and listened to Mother swish through the dining room. How would I get her to fix the sagging floorboards and flaking walls in the back bedroom before the house fell in altogether?

Since Daddy died, she'd been there by herself and let things go. "It makes me too nervous. Don't talk to me about it now." The usual response, whenever the subject was brought up, was now on automatic pilot in my head. Nagging didn't help and rationality was not a consideration, since that word must have been snipped from the big, dusty dictionary on the desk in the den long ago.

It had taken several weeks and quite a few headache-producing, arduous *two people talking at the same time* phone conversations to get Mother to agree to have somebody come and examine the multiplying holes in the wall that led into her bedroom. Some mornings, insects swarmed out of them into the surrounding hallway. Of course, I'd never seen them, only their artwork on the wall. But her description of being engulfed by flying ants when she got up to make breakfast made me worry.

This time, on the day I arrived, I saw evidence of a recent battle when I went to the back of the house to retrieve a sweater for her. The hall's dark hardwood floor was a nice backdrop for the copious remains of dead, willowy, translucent winged insects she swatted with a feather duster that was kept on top of the washing machine. They looked a lot like termites to me.

I knew we were in trouble when termite Bobby—so his nameplate said—came into the house. His manner betrayed his thoughts—Mother was old, probably deaf and certainly shouldn't be making these kinds of decisions. Never to look at her, only at me, when he talked was his first mistake. His grave was dug when, following an inspection, he revealed the truth in a scolding, pointed finger, lecture form—the house was in serious need of repair due to termite damage. The funeral was over with the announcement that it would cost more than the car she bought back in 1987 to become a model termite-proof homeowner—now looking straight at her, he used those exact words.

I had called the company, with Mother's reluctant blessing, the week before I arrived for my visit and planned to be there to hear the diagnosis firsthand when they came to take a look. The whole arrangement almost fell apart that morning over breakfast. She had her *I'm not going to listen to you so don't even think about it* face on when I came into the kitchen. Consequently, I wasn't the least surprised when she turned around from the stove and said, "I should never have let you organize this meeting. I'm not having people all over my house, stinking up everything with chemicals that'll smother me to death. You know how allergic I am to odors, and this is bound to kill me for sure. I've a good mind to go on over to Walmart before I have one of my spells. So, you might as well call him and cancel."

She slammed the dishwasher shut after filling it with dishes already scrubbed to a shine by hand in the sink, turned the dial to wash, and added, "And you'd better not tell him we're going to do anything without asking me first, either."

It took thirty minutes of groveling, pleading, and promising that this would just be a social call before she finally agreed to let him in. Now, he was dust in the road, never to be heard from again.

No more was said about termite Bobby. Tail dragging, I went home, two hundred miles away, to devise a new plan. Two months went by with no action. My hand had to be slapped several times to keep it from reaching for the phone, all caused by irrational thoughts of trying to coerce her into some kind of decision, until one day when the phone rang with what she described as "good news." She'd hired a man from up on Cosby who had already come by to take a look at the situation. He'd worked wonders for the cousin of somebody she met in the laxative aisle at Food City. No, she didn't know if he had a license and why did it matter, anyway? Apparently, he could do the job for a fraction of the cost and kill every flying ant in East Tennessee. That was the good news!

Now for the bad news! Even though he didn't plan to spray any chemicals, there would be some kind of pellets deposited around and under the house.

"Why, them pellets don't have no odor at all, and you'll never know we've been here," he told her.

But, of course, that wasn't true; she would smell them and would most likely be overcome by the fumes before we could get her to the hospital. Worrying through the night about who would feed the dogs if she died, she'd tried to cancel the project, but his phone number no longer worked, having been disconnected. After making several calls to "people that might know him," a new number was wrenched from the man who delivers hay to her farm. She reached the flying ant man's wife who assured her that nobody had died from the treatment yet. He would show up as planned.

But wait a minute, what about the dogs? The pellets will poison them, she feared. Several obsessive phone calls later, she was finally assured that the dogs would not expire from eating the pellets if penned up in the corner of the yard.

"This is just a bother. It's making me nervous just thinking about it. I've got to leave the house and go somewhere else. Why don't you come for a visit and stay until the job's done?" she asked. I decided to drive up there and stay three days. It would take the first day to calm her down before he started the work.

Then, on the second day during the fly slaughter, we'd go around to some of her favorite antique shops to look for carnival glass to add to her *every single space in the house covered* overflowing collection, then head on over in the late afternoon to spend the night at a local motel so that the anticipated atomic fog would have time to "get out of the curtains" before returning to the house the following day. That would be just long enough for the smell that wasn't a smell to go away, but only if all of the windows and doors in the house were cracked open wide enough to let it out.

"Nothing will get stolen while we're gone," she said. "I'll call the neighbors and tell them where we're going so they can be on the lookout in case something happens."

The third day, if all went well, we'd go down to the farm after breakfast so she could pet the *can't stand up by itself* lame calf she'd saved after it was hit by the car on the road that goes by the barn and see if the goats and chickens had been fed by the farmhand. Then we'd drive up to the Apple Barn to get some fried pies and sorghum, have lunch at Cracker Barrel, and be home by 2:00. It was a plan—one that might work.

Motel reservations made; panic struck as I remembered the last time I saw a suitcase in that house. It fell on my head out of the top shelf when I started to clean out the hall closet after Daddy died. All covered with mold and spider webs with corroded clasps, it got tossed into the trash without her knowing. She wouldn't have let go of it if I had asked, though it hadn't been taken from that shelf in more than twenty years, the last time they took an overnight trip anywhere.

How would she get her clothes to the motel? I called to ask if she wanted me to bring an extra suitcase, but that wouldn't be necessary. "It might have remnants of perfume in it from some trip you took. I'll just put my nightgown and underwear in a paper bag. That'll be fine," she said.

The flying ant man arrived at 9:00 a.m. sharp. "Now don't go in the house and touch my glass or move anything in my bedroom, you hear? And I'd better not come back and find one of those pellets on the back porch or in the yard where the dogs can get to it," she scolded.

"No, Ma'am. Me and the boys'll just put 'em under the house and inside the foundation. Don't you worry. You won't see or smell a thing." She double-checked the open windows and reminded him twice not to close the doors or windows when he got finished.

I put our overnight bags in the car and backed it slowly down the driveway and into unknown territory. I hadn't spent a night in a motel with her since 1963, and that was not a pleasant memory. That was the last trip I made with my parents to New Jersey, our annual vacation trek. It was a doozy, one filled with motel rooms in Virginia—coming and going—that had greasy bed linens, arguments over where to stop and eat, and certainty that a ghost was living at the relative's house where we were staying, causing us to return home a day early, since the lights kept coming on for no reason at all hours of the day and night.

Red sails in the sunset, we arrived at the motel after a day of antique browsing in Morristown and eating copious amounts of cafeteria-style food for lunch. The plan was going well. The flying ant man had been mentioned only once. "I paid him before we left, because I don't want him coming back to get the money with smelly clothes on after working in those chemicals all day," she said. "You remember how your daddy's clothes smelled when he got home from work at the nylon plant. Why that stuff killed him and will probably kill me eventually, since I washed all of those stinky clothes for thirty years," she said, ending with, "I like to pay up front. That way I know it'll be done right."

I parked under the covered entryway and went inside to get the room key and leave my credit card number with the desk clerk while Mother waited in the car. We had an outside room and parked right in front of the door. She liked that. "Well, I'm glad we found a close parking place. Now we can get to the car quick in case there's a fire," she said.

I took in the bags, checked out the towel and soap situation, and went into the bathroom for a few minutes while she stood in the doorway looking out across the field next to the motel. I heard her talking to somebody as I opened the bathroom door. I'd never seen them before. Must be tourists. One of the three people, standing just outside the room, asked how far it was from here to Walmart, Cracker Barrel, and several other places.

For the next ten minutes, Mother gave directions, plus names and descriptions of people who worked there, how long she'd known them and how many classes they had together in high school, so that the strangers could recognize them on sight.

She said, "You can't get good service there unless you know somebody."

The strangers finally moved on, but several more people walked by, all receiving a long-lost-friends greeting. She didn't want to close the door.

"It makes me feel claustrophobic. We may need to leave it open during the night," she said.

"We'll talk about that after dinner," I replied.

After a plastic meal in the motel restaurant, we stopped on the way back to the room at the refreshment area that held two Coke machines, the ice dispenser, and one vending machine that spit out candy bars, crackers, and other kinds of snacks. It was only 7:00 p.m. and we might get hungry later, so we bought three packages of peanut butter crackers and two Sprites just in case.

Mother finally settled down to watch *Jeopardy*, her favorite show, while I retreated to a small open room near the common area around the indoor pool to practice tai chi and try to exhale after holding my breath for two days. Feeling more relaxed, I got back to the room around 8:00 to find her in her nightgown, sitting up in bed, watching TV.

"I'll never sleep a wink. I know I won't," she complained, and got up to go into the bathroom as I undressed and started to take off my makeup. Two hours and three TV shows later, the crackers and Sprite disappeared into our stomachs. At least she hadn't mentioned the flying ant man since early afternoon.

At 10:00 p.m. I asked if she wanted me to turn off one of the bedside lamps. It was bright enough in that room to land a 747 at midnight. Her response was a surprise. She bolted upright in bed and started looking all around the room and rushed into the bathroom, her old, flimsy nightgown barely covering her backside.

"What's the matter, Mother?"

"Lord, where's my purse. You don't reckon I left it on top of the Coke machine, do you?"

It was not in the room. I pulled on my pants and shirt over my nightgown and said, "I'll go back down to the vending machines and see if I can find it."

"Lord, Lord, hurry up. It's got all that money in it," she said as my hand grabbed the doorknob.

"What money?" I asked, starting to panic, knowing that she had inherited my grandfather's disdain for banks and a habit of leaving too much cash lying around the house. "I might need a few dollars to buy food for the dogs," she'd say, when I chided her about it.

"I brought my dog money out of the desk in the pink bedroom."

"How much money, Mother?"

"Twenty thousand dollars, give or take. Now don't start," she said, looking defiant.

I didn't realize until later that I had forgotten to zip my pants, and my shirt was on backwards. I made it to the Coke machines in Olympic time and almost collided with two kids throwing a football on the sidewalk between our room and the alcove where the machines were housed. Breathless, I lurched into the glaring light of the refreshment center and spied the old, battered, brown purse, barely sitting, tilting over the edge of the vending machine to the left. I grabbed it, ripped it open and declared a miracle. There it was, an envelope with a two-inch-thick wad of money held together with a rubber band.

51

I stood in the machine-humming, fluorescent-blinding snack room for a long minute before returning slowly to Room 237 where mother stood in the doorway in her thin nightgown, backlit by the blaring TV.

"You mean it was still there?"

She took the purse, inspected the money, counted out every last dollar on the bed, put it all back together with the rubber band. Then, she stashed the purse behind the pillow on the chair by the door and said, "When we get home tomorrow, I'd better not find any evidence of those pellets around that house. If he didn't kill all those flying ants, I'm not having it done again 'cause I don't ever want to spend another night in this motel."

Cashed In

The contents of Poppa's dresser drawers were remarkably unlike his outer façade; a mirror into a dimension that no one knew existed. Several were stuck, swollen from excessive humidity and age. Once pried open, they spilled out odd, mismatched socks, unopened birthday cards and unused gifts from relatives or friends, piles of old and crumbly stamps, shirts with ripped sleeves, clumps of random buttons that surely belonged to someone else's clothes, and bits of cigars that had been chewed into points. It was all mashed together, a disintegrating compost heap of one man's life away from view.

He was Mother's daddy. She was the third oldest of six children and called him Poppa. He was Poppy to some of the others. When word started spreading that he was coming South, excited phone calls jingled from all corners of the county and one of the aunts or cousins would announce, "Poppy's coming down from New Jersey for the week." But that didn't sound right. To us, he was Poppa.

Poppa seldom came to our house, except for Christmas dinners or an occasional pass through town on his way to some other relative's house to spend the night, a week, or a month. He'd arrive in the afternoon, unceremoniously hand Mother a gift of carnival glass or a small piece of antique jewelry, look over the house and yard, pat the dogs, pass some time with Daddy talking about how the country was "going to Hell in a handbag," then sit at one end of the dining room table, Daddy at the other end, while we ate dinner mostly in silence, except for the clicking of Daddy's off-kilter jaw when he chewed and Poppa's smacking lips that occasionally emitted exclamations about the feast. I sat to his right. Mother never really sat at all, rushing back and forth into the kitchen to retrieve more delicacies that no one could eat for lack of space on our plates or in our overfilled waistbands.

We didn't see him much when I was a child. He spent more time with Mother's brothers and sisters or travelling, doing whatever Poppas do when they have the freedom to do it. When he did occupy space in our corner of town, conversations with Poppa were limited to the copious amounts of food Mother prepared, the weather, and the trip from New Jersey—detailed around views of Skyline Drive, his Staunton, Virginia lodgings, and the confusing traffic in Washington, D.C—places we all knew, having seen them on our treks up the map by the same route. If there were other conversations with Poppa, they didn't include me. So, he was a mystery I never solved.

We never knew for sure when Poppa would arrive. Frantic calls went back and forth between the sisters and cousins until everyone had pinned down exactly the time Poppa would be at a certain house for supper on any given night. As soon as Mother got the news, a cooking frenzy took hold of her that lasted until his car cranked up, left our little hill, and headed toward his next familial conquest. Two cakes and a pie had to be made: a chocolate cake with caramel icing; a seven-layer stack cake—each cookie dough layer rolled out and baked on the back of a round cake pan—filled with simmered dried apples, sugar, and butter that turned into a smooth applesauce spread thickly between the cake rounds and left to sit covered up in Saran Wrap for at least two days until it was soft and melted in your mouth; and a chocolate cream pie with three-inch high meringue that never fell nor wept—it had been her mother's recipe and the one Poppa liked best.

Besides the three desserts, there were three meats: a baked ham, Swiss steak, and fried chicken; two salads, lettuce tossed with tiny tomatoes in a light vinaigrette dressing and an orange congealed one with cream cheese and pineapple topping; at least four vegetables, sometimes more—green beans cooked with ham, creamed corn, broccoli, peas, a squash casserole, and soup beans and sliced tomatoes; corn bread and rolls.

Poppa commanded attention. Once the time of his arrival was established, preparation details multiplied with haste. Mother's hand needed to touch everything that would touch his and no one else was allowed to assist for fear of mistakes that Poppa would notice. On the breathtaking day of his ascent to our house, I was a lookout, stationed at the front door to announce his arrival while Mother put the finishing touches to the food and the table.

The long, sleek, pale yellow Lincoln Continental he drove wouldn't fit in our driveway. Instead, he parked it across the street in the neighbor's detached garage to avoid the inevitable sideswipe by passing cars that whirred around the corner on the winding road in front of our house. We'd watch as he rested it in its stall after long trips out in the country or down to see one of his two (didn't-know-each-other-existed-until-his-funeral) lady-friends who lived miles away from each other in two different directions. Upon his death, its trunk revealed years of unopened gifts from these two estranged confidants—expensive rings and watches, cashmere sweaters, shirts and ties, wallets, even an elaborately carved jewelry box—that made us speculate whether they ever wondered what happened to their generosity once given. None of these worship offerings had ever been exposed to light outside the closed lid nor removed from their original boxes or wrappings to be complimented by passing acquaintances or touch the skin of one so admired.

Poppa had a remarkable presence. He was tall and solidly built. A thick shock of coarse paper-white hair with natural waves set off dark bespectacled eyes and a sandy complexion, reminiscent of black-and-white-movie stars of the 30s and 40s. Not just on Sunday, he wore tailored suits or neatly pressed suspendered linen dress pants and rolled-up long-sleeved shirts in pastel colors that made his smooth, wrinkleless skin look like the young man he wasn't.

When he went downtown, his long stride circled block by block, until an unmistakable scent marked every corner from the courthouse to the Coffee Pot café. All conversation stopped when he came into a room or glided by a window. Women gazed at his back a little too long and the men chummed up to match his pace, trying to catch hold of the free-flowing, money-giving, no-bother-to-get-an–IOU generosity that defined him.

When I graduated from high school and went farther south to college, Mother spoke of freedom to do all the things she'd wanted to do, but that didn't last long when Poppa's decision was made to take up residence on the hill with my parents, the antique glass, and the dogs. Once my room was empty and Poppa came back to Newport to stay for a while, he never again left for long. I would see him only at Christmas holidays and in the summer when I sailed through for short visits.

I had told George, my college boyfriend who later became my husband, that Poppa lived with my parents now that I was in college. But I didn't tell him that Poppa was full of surprises.

George arrived on a steamy summer afternoon, his first visit to my house since we'd been dating. He'd met my parents the Christmas before when they picked me up in Chattanooga, where I'd spent a few days with his family. Now, he was parked in the den with Poppa until dinner was ready. Daddy still at work, Mother and I in the kitchen, George sat on the couch while Poppa gestured at the blaring TV news and solved all the world's problems with the statement, "Just mow 'em all down."

"Want a little nip, boy?" Poppa asked through a cigar-smoke cloud that hung around the wooden arm of the orange-and-brown-speckled rocker he'd made his own after arriving in Newport for what he called "a short stay" some two years before. At the beginning of June 1965, he took over the corner rocker—the one Daddy's backside had made an impression in—next to the outside door in the den. Now, when he wasn't at work, Daddy spent most of his time on the back porch with the dogs, smoking Camels until supper was ready or until Poppa had vacated his favorite chair to read or get ready for bed right after he ate supper.

"Sir?" George leaned in to hear him a little better, not knowing what he meant.

"Want a little nip?" Poppa barked as he nimbly lifted his more than seventy-five-year-old, six-foot, sturdy frame from its confines, motioned for George to follow him down the hall and took off.

Once inside my growing-up-years blue bedroom—where he had relocated a few shirts, pants, and money clip from New Jersey, just after I removed fourteen boxes of shoes, three hats, a dozen belts, and more outfits than the dorm room could hold at the college in Florida—he parted the sliding wooden doors to the closet and reached down for a mason jar filled with what looked like sparkling, clear water. Several sizes of moonshine-filled mason jars were lined up neatly around the closet floor and represented payback for money loaned to sad souls amid bad times met on jaunts through town or out to farmland he owned on the other side of the county. Real cash-money rarely surfaced from those loans, but Poppa didn't seem to need it or care.

He took two small crystal glasses from the top of his dresser, filled each to the brim, shoved one in George's hand and said, "Boy, one of these in the mornin' and one in the evenin' and you'll live as long as I have. Now drink up." The coughing and sputtering brought us out of the kitchen to find Poppa laughing at the top of his voice and George red-faced and unable to speak, having downed his first slug of straight moonshine in one gulp as directed by the master.

Over the next ten years or so of marriage, graduate school, a move across the state, and visits only on holidays, George and I rarely saw Poppa. An elusive figure, he came and went at will from my parent's house until age and sickness took its toll and I found myself at his funeral in the late 70s where it was plain to see that his large, extended brood would be more fractured without the excitement and anticipation of his time with them. The hushed conversation was solemn but filled with wonder at what he was really like, where he had really been, and how much he was really worth. Each relative or friend drew a "They!" (East Tennessee for "I'm surprised at that") or a "You don't say!" reaction to a story about some side of Poppa that no one else recognized. So, the most overheard comment was, "Poppa was full of surprises."

It had been a few weeks since Poppa's funeral, the time filled with details, questions, and chaos among the clan. He left no will, and his children were in disarray about what to do with his belongings and properties he owned in two states. Mother had avoided Poppa's room, swearing she had seen him in there late one night shortly after he died, and felt no inclination to remove any of his belongings until she became the executor of his estate.

But, one day a few weeks after the funeral, she came down the hall with a broom, dust cloths, small trashcan, and several tools and announced to Daddy that they needed to clean out the closet and get those drawers in the dresser unstuck. Anything they found would be divided up among the relatives or given away to charity.

Mother didn't keep many remembrances of Poppa, just his sturdy cane with its carved deer head on the top and his pocket watch that she stationed on a wire hanger inside an antique glass dome. To keep it company, a small antique hand painted porcelain box nestled next to it on the round walnut finished wooden base. The cane leaned against an old rocking chair and the watch sat on the dresser in the blue bedroom until she died when they came home with me.

When they began to unravel the contents of the blue bedroom that Poppa and I had inhabited, it revealed bits of both of us that were embedded in creaky, old-smelling drawers or shoved into dusty closet shelves, things that had taken up cozy residence without fear of being forgotten—old 45 rpms of Elvis, Little Richard, and Jerry Lee Lewis—complete with a workable turntable, small crocheted doll dresses for the only two dolls I ever noticed and had long dismissed, trophies from piano competitions and baton twirling festivals and parts of letters that didn't match on pieces of notebook paper from school tablets that were stained and unreadable, and a menagerie of stuffed animals that spent years waiting in speculation about whether I would return. That was the predictable, leftover life from my childhood in that space.

But Poppa had left some surprises. Though the closet held the elegant clothes and several quarts of moonshine that Mother insisted had to be flushed down the toilet, his old dresser revealed a curiosity that no one could have imagined and spilled out contents that set my parents on a course of hard work, tedium, laughter, and awe.

"Where is everybody?" I yelled as George and I came into the den from the driveway, having just arrived for a visit, finding no one and hearing no sound in the house. Then a faint voice responded from a distance.

"We're in the kitchen."

We walked down the long hall past the blue-walled bedroom with flounced curtains and matching blue bedspread on the right and the frilly pink bedroom on the left, past the phone nook and the organ stool, the antique cabinets filled with one-of-kind pieces of carnival and other old glassware, through the 60s-style living room, and around the corner into the dining room with its blonde furniture and gleaming, never-used "good" china as Mother called out, "You won't believe what we found."

I had never seen my parents working together so perfectly in sync. It was obvious they had a plan and were determined to execute it, something I was unused to when I was living at home.

We stopped dead at the kitchen door. Daddy, in a short-sleeved shirt, held what looked like money under the running water in the kitchen sink. Our eyes took in the mounds of bills piled in stacks side-by-side on every inch of counter space and top of the square, blue-speckled table that grounded the center of the kitchen.

"It took a hammer and a chisel, but I finally got that top drawer of Poppa's dresser open," Daddy said, handing Mother another clump of wet bills.

"You mean all of this money was in there?" George asked, trying to surmise just how much was laid out in front of us.

"Lord, when we got it open, all of this was gaumed up and stuck together with cough syrup that had spilled out a long time ago. It was the biggest mess I've ever seen," said Mother as she dried off the bills with a dishrag and placed them neatly into stacks.

"We had to take damp cloths in there and pry 'em off one bill at a time to get 'em out without tearing 'em," Daddy added.

"Now we're having to wash 'em, one at a time, and then put 'em in stacks according to value," Mother said as we stared at the mountains of cash growing by inches as they worked.

"I always knew Poppa didn't trust banks, but I had no idea he was keeping this kind of money around the house," I said, picking up a stack of hundred-dollar bills.

"How much do you think is here?" George asked, almost in a whisper, as if someone on the back porch would hear him.

"Aw, I'd say around fifteen to twenty thousand, take or leave," Daddy replied with a laugh. "No wonder he always had money falling out of his pockets for every Tom, Dick, and Harry that tapped his shoulder."

"Well, I hope it was cleaner than this when he gave it to them," said Mother.

"I sure never thought you'd be in the business of money laundering," I said, flipping through a four-inch stack of tens.

Poppa was indeed full of surprises!

Pitched

Daddy died on a Tuesday in April. I wasn't there.

It was 1:37 a.m. Central Time when the phone shocked me out of an ill-fitting sleep. Mother was at home in East Tennessee, five hours away from me and two blocks from the hospital where Daddy had been taken by the farmhand who'd been at the house the past week sitting up with him as he thrashed through the nights. She was having one of her spells. Too nervous to go to the hospital, she said. "Can't you come on up here? He might be going to die."

It had been eight days since Daddy began seeing squirrels in the closet. Mother had laughed when she told me about it. But I knew she was worried. I mentioned it, jokingly, when I called him the following day to see how he was getting on, knowing how he was getting on, unable to walk or go to the bathroom by himself, hard knots on his elbows and wrists and the bottoms of his feet, gnarled fingers so painful that he couldn't grip a glass or pick up a book and bouts of colitis that required Depends. He swore he'd use that gun hidden in the old secretary in the den if he had the strength to pull the trigger. He didn't remember seeing squirrels.

Ninety pounds is too little for a man of five feet eight inches to weigh. He'd shrunk forward and leaned sideways as he walked. Unable to flex toes nor ankles or keep his misshapen feet from turning out, he shuffled along, arms dangling in asymmetrical positions from bony shoulders that stuck out through the new shirts I bought him for Christmas.

"I'll try to get there tomorrow, Mother," I said, picturing all the times I'd failed to convince them to get a second opinion about his health, go down to Knoxville and see a "real" doctor, or get a nurse to come in and stay with him at night. It had been a mostly downhill slide for nine years. I dreaded every visit, never knowing what to expect: weight gain or loss, bumped-up energy on Prednisone, improved appetite with a string of days when the bathroom was not a dreaded place, or confinement to the faded rust-colored rocker in the den, too frail to get up and eat. Angry about what life had done to him, his eyes betrayed the constant crushing pain and the loss of control.

Daddy—who used to smoke two packs of unfiltered cigarettes a day, eat Spam sandwiches on light bread, and drive a Honda Civic that was rusted out by toxic fumes coming out of smokestacks at the nylon plant where he worked—said that if he ever had to go back down to that hospital he'd never come out alive. I guess he was right.

Reviewing and preparing, I waited in the dark bedroom for the phone to ring, my husband next to me, resigned to a long drive the next morning. The call came an hour later. Mother's voice was shaky, barely audible. "They should have paid more attention," she said. The news had come from a night nurse she'd seen just yesterday buying pantyhose down at Food City. Apparently, he swallowed his tongue and choked. Mother didn't know if they tried to revive him. The doctor never came by to see Daddy and the farmhand left before midnight.

The death certificate states he died of pneumonia with rheumatoid arthritis listed as a complementary ailment. I doubt he would like the sound of that. In the nine years since a doctor at the plant told him he'd have to quit and take disability because he was just going to get worse, there'd been nothing *complimentary* about it.

He retired early, parked the Honda in the side yard, rarely saw his old friends and only left the house to go to the grocery store and places Mother thought up: antique malls, junk shops, and a yearly drive through the dogwood trails around Maryville. As time passed, the trips became scarce and were limited to the short drive down to the farm he inherited from his aunt. Barely able to walk, he rarely got out of the car, just sat and looked at the place from the side road next to the old barn with hay falling out of the loft. Daddy spent most days on the back porch with the stray dogs that came to the house. They outlived him, every single one.

His regular doctor told him to quit smoking and drinking coffee, the only two things that seemed to make his life bearable. He got down to three cigarettes a day, one after every meal. He smoked them outside with the dogs because mother wouldn't let him smoke in the house anymore. They gave her sick headaches, she said.

Giving up the coffee was never a consideration. He drank it black; four hot cups at breakfast, three cold ones between breakfast and dinner when a fresh pot was made and finished off before bedtime. It wasn't the caffeine that kept him awake, he insisted.

He'd delayed going to the hospital this time by several needed days because he knew they'd cut off his coffee. He was sixty-six and two blocks from home: no farmhand, no doctor, no family.

We drove up I-40 and got to their house late in the afternoon. The Central Time Zone ceases somewhere around Rockwood causing an uncomfortable body shift. Everything seems late on Eastern Time. It's hard to catch up. The evening news comes on the TV late. The sun sets late, and hunger always arrives about an hour before dinner.

Some of the neighbors were already there crowded around the piano in the living room. Mother got teary when they talked about how I had her dimples and Daddy's brown-green eyes. As they went out the front door, they all declared what a shame it was that he had to suffer so long. We were left to meander the long hardwood halls and silent rooms of the big ranch-style house filled with gold-flecked carnival glass, antique tables and bureaus, and a rounded glass-front secretary Daddy and the dogs had refinished some years back.

We mulled the farewell. What kind would it be? Appearances. Expectations. Daddy drove four blocks out of the way around any church he might have to go into, so there would be no funeral, no viewing, no preacher, just a short graveside service. "That's what he'd want," Mother said. Crowds made her nervous.

My husband and I, professional musicians with advanced music degrees that Mother had bragged about, knew what was coming. "Could you sing something?" she asked, looking meek and pale, as we considered our options.

Maybe we should record it. No, too artificial. The service would be outdoors; thus, no piano and it had been years since either of us had played the only three chords we knew on the guitar. It was certain my voice would falter since I'm known for crying all the way through ET even though I've seen it seven times. So, Mother looked up at my husband, who said smilingly, "I'll be glad to sing something *a cappella* and say a few words about him."

Relief! She seemed satisfied, but...could he please sing Daddy's favorite song, one we'd never heard of and had no idea where to find? Apparently not. "Amazing Grace" was a good substitute.

An only child is the one responsible. So, I started making a list of all tasks that had to be done, similar to the day I got married, when I was still checking things off and sewing one of the bridesmaids into her dress fifteen minutes before the wedding.

The next two days were a blur of buying real estate—they had no gravesites—picking out the casket, it had to be a certain kind and color, inside and out, according to Mother, though no one would see the inside—filling out forms and paying bills for the funeral home services, a most shocking transaction that cost more than my parents paid for their house and lot in 1952. I have the bill of sale.

The hospital called. Daddy's belongings could be picked up at the nurse's station on the main floor. "Are you the next of kin?" asked the nurse just before she disappeared into the next room. A pair of old pants, a checkered shirt and undershirt, a thin, misshapen wallet and a pair of worn black nylon socks, his favorites, were inside a large black garbage bag that was tossed over the counter. I don't remember taking the bag to the car.

"He should have worn a clean shirt down there," said mother when she took everything out of the bag and laid it on the bed. The bag was just the right size for the garbage can outside the kitchen door. We never spoke of it again.

Mother decided to wear a pale pink pants suit and looked smaller than usual, a tiny five feet four in beige pumps with grosgrain bows. I wore black with sunglasses and my husband had on a white shirt, hand painted silk tie, and dark suit. He's known for his charismatic speaking and musical talent. So, we left the house on a cool, sunny morning and drove six blocks to the cemetery feeling confident that we'd get to a satisfactory end of this dreaded necessity.

Mother was pleased when she saw the two plots. "How nice that there's a good view of the Smokies," she said as we approached the gathering. We had done well.

A few people were sitting quietly, staring toward the shiny gray casket covered with mounds of white, pink, and lavender blossoms that trailed over the sides. Sympathy sprays and baskets of flowers were placed on either side and in the back. There was a lone shefflera sent by someone who must have had another event in mind. It leaned a little left, had few leaves on the right side and badly needed water, a sign that the out-of-town customer had paid too much and wasn't planning to attend.

It was a small gathering: a few neighbors, no relatives on either side of the family except my mother and me. The farmhand sat in a chair placed outside and to the left of the funeral home tent. He apologized later for not having time to clean up.

Greetings exchanged, the funeral book signed, Mother and I sat down on the front row. After a moment of silence, the clear, resonant, reassuring voice of Daddy's son-in-law began to speak of him, recalling his attributes and pastimes, interspersed with poetry, the 23rd Psalm and a sprinkle of humor. Mother 's eyes were wet as she smiled over at me approvingly. The eulogy had been prepared without my interaction, so it was gratifying to hear such an agreeable delivery.

Ten minutes into the service is a good place for a song. I didn't know exactly when the song would be sung but being a singer myself and knowing my husband's mannerisms, I felt it was about that time. He cleared his throat after reading the poem, made a point to stand up a little taller so that breathing could be at its peak for making tones, and announced that one of Daddy's favorite songs was "Amazing Grace." He swallowed deliberately, looked down at his black folder and waited a long minute before starting.

Some people have perfect pitch. I don't have it. Neither does he. But good relative pitch is all one really needs and perhaps a pitch pipe, which no one thought of before coming to the service. So, good relative pitch would have to suffice as it had many times before.

There is a thing called "singer's empathy." Some singers have it and others don't. I have it. If I'm in the audience and a singer is having difficulty of any kind, maybe a frog in the throat, not enough breath to make it to the end of a phrase, or inability to hit the high note, I respond as if I'm the one doing the singing. Tension creeps into every sinew of my throat and body preparing for the inevitable crash.

It was the swallow that gave me pause. Not normal, I thought. But I chose to ignore it.

The first two notes of the song were a surprise to me. I knew they were a surprise to him as well, without looking in that direction—I dared not look.

A bystander at the scene of an accident—I looked.

At first, the tones were secure, though a bit shrill, and at least a fourth too high in pitch. I adjusted my sunglasses and looked hard at the corner pole holding up the pale gray tent. Having sung "Amazing Grace" dozens of times, I anticipated the inevitable. There was no way to escape the fact that this normally suave baritone voice would soon be approaching high notes that only the infamous *castrati* could have achieved with ease. It's much like starting to cross a bridge as it divides in two and rises for the oncoming ship to go under, pure panic at reaching the peak with nowhere to go.

I can recall only a few times when appropriate public decorum was difficult for me to achieve. For instance, that time at the symphony premiere when the tenor soloist was bellowing about being the engine of a plane crossing the ocean and the chorus sang repeatedly in response, "Do you have any gas?" In pain from holding in the laughter, I feigned a cough, left quickly by the side door, and convulsed for several minutes when I hit the ladies' room across the hall.

This was going to be one of those times. How many lines are there in this song?

Amazing Grace. OK, just. The day wasn't hot enough for that much perspiration.

How Sweet the Sound. Not quite. A nervous shake had developed in the tone. Another quick swallow in recognition of the impending *That Saved a Wretch Like Me.* He had reached customs and just remembered his passport was still in the bureau drawer.

Muscles tightened just under the jaw, the chin lifted slightly, and the breath came a bit too quickly, pulling in rather than expanding outward. I don't know what *he* was doing. I didn't look.

Thank God for falsetto! Baritones usually have good ones and this one had been used a lot. Whew!

The gear shift was even, but unexpected. Unfortunately, it had to be maintained for *I Once was Lost.* Was that a trill or a quiver? One more swallow came just before the tone cracked into a yodel. Several heads looked up. Who knew Daddy liked this version better than the original?

But Now I'm Found, city limits and just enough gas to get home. Look over the heads, never in the eyes and cruise through to *Was Blind but Now I See.*

This song was longer than I remembered. No reason to hang on to that last note.

I was riveted to that sleek coffin. Sunglasses bored into my nose, toes pulled in and pressed down hard, and mouth held tightly clamped so that if a laugh escaped it would seem like a sympathetic whimper to those around me.

"Let Us Now Go in Peace," he said after a short prayer.

Hugs. Kisses. Cars leaving. Waves.

The funeral book was closed and given to Mother. Had everybody signed? Each name was reviewed while the sun tinted her pale skin red.

As we started toward the car, Mother turned for one last look at the flowers. "I've never seen such a big spray on a casket." She patted my husband's arm, thanked him for all the kind things he said about Daddy and ended earnestly, "Now don't you worry about that song. I didn't give you enough time to practice."

Daddy's funeral brings an unexpected smile every time my mind goes there. It was pitch perfect.

Animal Attraction

"Are you there?"

Silence.

"I know you're there!" the caller insisted.

The familiar voice shouted from the tiny, ancient cassette that recorded incoming messages and had never been replaced since buying the answering machine some ten years before. This was long before cell phones became the norm. This baby-sized cassette must have been made of an indestructible material found only on Pluto and kept secret by the company that had produced it. If only other much-needed items like hairdryers, washing machines, and light bulbs could last so long.

The message emitting from the bedroom side table was anticipated since her calls always began that way. Mother didn't really need to ask the question. It didn't matter if I was actually there or not, since in her mind—no matter the time of day or night—I was most definitely there and simply chose not to respond to her calls.

Some days I would come home from a long day at work and find several messages from her—ones that lasted to the very end of the limit allowed for leaving messages. When cut off in mid-sentence, she would redial, begin with her usual, "I know you're there," and take up where she left off until the time ran out again. Thus, it might take four or five message segments on the machine to vent whatever was on her mind that day. This might go on for thirty minutes or more and cause me to dread what lay ahead when I saw the flashing message light beckoning.

On one particular late afternoon, I was working in my office at the far end of the house when the phone rang. Not wanting to interrupt my train of thought, I decided to screen the call just in case it was the local cemetery—though, after receiving several calls from them offering me a discount rate on a perfect plot for my remains, I had told them my plans to be cremated and have my ashes dropped over the Metropolitan Opera in New York City. It had been more than a month since their last call.

Just as I reached the door to the bedroom, the voice said, "I know you're there, so pick up. You won't believe what I'm looking at."

Some pesky, uncontrollable urge came over me and I grabbed the phone.

"Hi," I said and explained that I was in the midst of grading papers and had only a few minutes to talk. I could have ended my greeting with "Hi." The papers would be yellow and flaking with neglect, age, and too little humidity before I saw them again, I feared.

"Well, what do you think I'm looking at?"

"I have no idea. Do you want me to guess?" I asked, sitting down in the chair next to the phone. As it turned out, sitting was a good idea.

It was six o'clock Eastern time—her time in East Tennessee—when she called and was already dark there. That nasty daylight savings time didn't agree with her. She liked light as long as she could get it in the afternoon.

"Go ahead and guess, but you'll never guess it."

After several random guesses that included visiting relatives, new carnival glass acquisitions, and one of her favorite TV shows, she said, "You're not even close."

"Alright, I give up. What are you looking at?"

"It's a possum," she said with a slight giggle. I assumed she was looking out the window and wondered why this was of interest since possums were a common sight in her neighborhood. Too often they were seen only after being run over and dragged to the side of the road in front of her house.

"Is it in your front yard?" A question I regretted just as it left my mouth. This was my mother calling about a possum. Of course, it was not in her front yard.

"No, no, no. Why would I call if it was in my front yard? That's silly," she scoffed.

"It's right here looking at me."

"You mean it's on the back porch?" Again, I had failed the test and knew it instantly when she said, "No, young'un"—a term she used to address me even though I was well over forty "— "it's sitting in my chair at the kitchen table drinking out of my coffee cup."

"What? How on earth did it get in? You did get that backdoor screen replaced, didn't you?" Even I didn't recognize my high-pitched, shrill voice. But there it was.

Mother didn't like to be reminded that things needed to be fixed around the house. There had been an ongoing effort to get a new screen for the kitchen door that led out onto a small concrete patio. She wouldn't have it fixed and wouldn't let me get it fixed. It had been one of several battles over decaying portions of her house that had become all too common since my father died a few years before. She didn't like change.

With each trip there, I saw more and more evidence that the house might someday simply disappear into crumbling dust and leave her standing in the middle. Prodding only seemed to make her more stubborn at the thought of repairs. But after much begging, she'd waved goodbye at the end of my last visit with a promise to call the local building supply store to have the door replaced. That had been more than two months ago.

The screen door she refused to let go of had been there since the late 60s and suffered jumping, scratching, and pawing from several generations of dogs. It was now barely hanging onto its frame, twisted so that it was hard to latch, and had holes in the screen at the bottom, though none were large enough to let a possum get through. In the summertime, the kitchen was exposed by its lack of a barrier from outside visitors. The neighborhood gnats and flies took long vacations there.

Mother's lapse into disarray had come as a surprise. This was the woman who—when I was growing up—dusted everything obsessively, washed green beans until they shined before cooking them, and daily replaced every knickknack, book, footstool, pillow, doll, throw rug, or pencil that might have been moved even an inch during the day. Nothing was allowed to be out of place or look less than sparkling at all times. She kept a perfect house and was congratulated for that by everyone who came to visit. Now, there was a possum sitting at her kitchen table drinking out of her coffee cup. How did this happen?

"Now don't start," she said. "It couldn't get in through the kitchen door. I've had it latched all day, except when I went out to feed the dogs and I always make sure to close it when I come back inside."

"Well, how do you think it got in?"

"It came out of the closet, I guess," she said, as if that was its usual home.

"What do you mean it came out of the closet? What closet?" I asked, leaning into the chair a little harder.

"Oh, I forgot to tell you about hearing the noise in the blue bedroom the other night. I went in there with my flashlight in case I needed to knock something in the head and heard scratching around inside the closet. When I opened the door, there were all of these little eyes looking back at me from the corner behind Poppa's clothes." These were clothes that still hung where my grandfather left them when he died in the late 70s.

"It was a mother possum and her babies," she said proudly. "My man on the farm drove up yesterday and got them out. He found a big hole in the back of the closet where they had come up through the floorboards and made a nest there, I reckon."

"Oh, my goodness. Then, where did this one come from?" I asked, feeling suddenly more tired than usual from our normal discourse.

"I guess it was already loose somewhere else in the house when he got here and hid when it heard him. It must have come out to get something to drink. I'm trying to figure out how to get it back outside," she said at a distance from the phone receiver.

"What are you doing now?" I asked, wondering if she was approaching the thing and fearful that it might jump up and cause her to fall.

"Well, I'm going to open the door to the patio and see if it'll go on out. Talk to me here for a few minutes so we can see if it'll go off by itself or if it needs a little help. OK?"

"Sure," I sighed, surmising that my papers would not get graded that day. While she kept her eyes on the intruder, we talked about how to make soup beans, how much hay it took to feed the cattle since there was a drought, the fact that one of our cousins hadn't eaten solid food and only drunk coffee for several years making it remarkable she was still alive, and Mother's disappointment that I had given up being a concert pianist for a career in singing since they spent all of that money on piano lessons when I was growing up—a topic we would discuss until the day she died, with no resolution.

After more than thirty minutes of psychological one-upmanship, with interjections about the current status of the possum, she whispered, "It's looking towards the door. I've got my broom. I'm going to see if I can shoo it out."

I whispered back, "Well, don't get too close or it might bite you."

She laid the phone down with a soft clunk onto the phone stand and was gone for several minutes while I worried that this would have a bad ending. I could hear her voice in the distance saying, "Get on out of here."

Then the screen door slammed with a bang, followed by the wooden door. Finally, she picked up the phone and said, "You know what, that rascal drank every drop of coffee in that cup. I didn't know they even liked coffee, did you?"

Take that Back

"Is there anything you need at the mall? I'm taking these pants back to Dillards. I tried them on and they're way too big," said the alien life form that had invaded my husband's body and was wearing his clothes. He carried a large shopping bag and was picking up car keys from the kitchen table. He sounded a little giddy.

Stunned, I asked, "You're what? You're going to take them back by yourself?"

This was a scene that I couldn't imagine ever happening in my lifetime. The alien was so like him that I started to believe he was really my husband. But that just couldn't be true. This was not the man who had always frowned and turned pale when I suggested shopping of any kind. From the beginning of our marriage, I had always bought his clothes, brought them home for him to try on, and would take anything back that didn't fit. Being an off-the-rack kind of person, he was easy to shop for and always wore the same size. He liked the colors and styles I picked out for him so rarely did things have to be taken back. It was a perfect arrangement. I loved to shop, and he had an obvious phobia about it, stating that he got lost in Lovemans department store in Chattanooga when he was a little boy and was sure his mother tried to leave him there.

He declared that shopping malls and department stores made him dizzy as soon as he entered the front door of one. When we were first married, he did go with me—which was not often—but would look anxious, ask how long it would take, stalk outside the store, read on a bench, or sit in the car while I picked up things inside. So, to alleviate anxiety on both parts, I learned that it was best if I went by myself or with friends. We could both exhale and enjoy life. Our shopping habits had happily remained intact for many years.

"I can't believe this. Are you sure you don't need me to take them back?" I said feeling upended by this change of habit. I had purchased the pants the day before and assumed that I would be taking them back, as usual.

"No, I think I've got the routine now. I think I'll look for some socks and a new shirt while I'm there. See you in a little while," he said, waving goodbye as the front door closed.

This alien was good.

At this point, the idea that he would ever go voluntarily into a mall by himself and look for clothes was ludicrous. He wasn't a browser. If he had to go to a store to buy tennis balls or a garden hose, he would go for just that thing, know exactly where it was in the store before going, go straight to it, buy it, and leave as his palms began to sweat.

Returning something that had been bought by either of us was even more anxiety ridden for him. It was unimaginable that he had ever entertained the idea of returning anything without several years of therapy to prepare for the occasion. If he bought a piece of clothing that didn't fit or a tool or appliance that didn't work, I would always return it. He had never returned anything in his life and had plead guilty to ignorance of the ritual and professed that I was the one who should make all returns due to an inherited take-back gene from my mother.

My growing up years were a blur of store packages—some rectangular cardboard boxes, others flimsy bags—that came and went, decorating the living room couch or my parents' bed. My mother did not like department store dressing rooms, claimed they were too small, the mirrors made her look fat, and the lighting caused her skin to appear sallow. I suspect she was more inclined toward claustrophobia. Thus, she never tried on clothes at the store. She would pick out something, buy it, bring it home, then let it sit in plain view for several days before trying it on. If it didn't fit or she found the color "off," as she would remark, the ill-fated garment would be taken back to the store for a refund. Mother's take-back talents didn't apply solely to clothing. Bath towels, rugs, bedspreads, mirrors, dishes, cooking utensils, and decorator items came and went as if they were in a holding pattern to their next destination and never meant to be in our house. I felt sorry for some of them because I knew they were so unattractive that no one would ever take them home for keeps.

I accompanied her on most of these take-back trips and—as a child—thought this was just a part of ordinary life and that everyone bought things this way. As I grew older, I realized that I enjoyed trying things on in the store and rarely had to take clothes back. But my early training on how to do it made the process easy when I needed to do it for myself or my husband. It was second nature by the time I graduated from college and got married. I had learned how to talk to salesclerks, how to follow the rules and how to break them from the master of take-back.

Our small town had a few excellent, locally owned stores that we frequented. I noticed that in the early days Mother always had the sales slip for the return, but as the years passed sometimes Mother had the sales slip and sometimes she didn't when returns were made. Apparently, by the time I married and moved away, it no longer mattered because everyone seemed to know my mother and apparently if she said she bought it there, then she bought it there.

As Mother aged, she continued her take-back routine but bought less of everything except tops and pants from department store sale racks that piled up on her bed and were never tried on nor returned to the store. She had added nothing new to her kitchen in several years. The look of her shelves and counter tops was exactly the same each time we visited.

As I watched my husband's car leave the driveway, I had a mental flash of what might have inspired him to break his mold. We had just returned from visiting my mother—who now lived alone following my father's death.

We arrived at her house in the early afternoon two days before Christmas and found her in the kitchen preparing dinner for seven, even though there would just be the three of us. We stood in the kitchen door making small talk as she cut up vegetables, pulled out the iron skillet to make fried chicken, and refused to let us help with anything, as usual. Needing to open a can of corn, she turned to the counter behind her and plugged in a can opener. It was a new Rival can opener, not the old rusted, banged up Rival can opener that she had used for the past eight or nine or who knows how many years and sounded like it was destined for the trash bin the last time we were there. I had offered to buy her a new one, but she wouldn't have it, saying, "This thing should last ten more years."

"Mother, you have a new can opener," I said, surprised to see that she had replaced the old one. She had refused to buy new appliances, large or small, for the past forty years and used the same pots and pans she'd had since getting married, certain that food would not taste the same in anything new.

"I came in here to plug it in last week and it wouldn't work at all. I can't believe that thing quit working. It should have lasted a lot longer," she said with a sigh as the opener ground around the top of the can.

"Where did you get this one?" I asked.

"Well, I took the old one back to Parks-Belk where I bought it, and would you believe they don't sell Rival anymore? I didn't want some off-brand, so I went out to Walmart and set that thing down on the counter and said, 'this can opener should have lasted a lot longer than it did. It won't even start up now. I need to swap it out for a new one.' So, they apologized and gave me one just like it— which they should have done—and it runs like a top."

On the way to our bedroom, we looked at each other and laughed out loud. Only my mother could take back something, maybe ten years old, to a place she didn't buy it and get a new one free.

I turned away from the front door knowing that my husband would be set for life now that he had been exposed to the best training anyone could ever have from the queen of take-back.

The Fix-It Gene

"What do you mean, you're sick?" Mother asked, peering around the front seat to find me sprawled out across the back seat of the '49 Ford that was barreling down Highway 11E toward Knoxville.

"I feel like I'm gonna throw up," I mumbled, holding tight to my new red patent leather purse, one I'd begged for every time we passed by it in the window at McNabb's Department store on Main Street in Newport. I figured that if I mentioned it enough times someone would surely take the hint and it would magically appear next to the chocolate layer cake with caramel icing I had requested for my tenth birthday. My theory had worked. Here I lay clutching it with all my might trying not to jiggle too much in case the syrupy pancake and bacon breakfast I'd eaten two hours earlier decided to end up on the red patent leather shoes that matched the new purse.

"Now keep your eyes looking forward like we talked about and sit up straight. Don't lay down on the seat. That'll just make it worse," she said, turning back around as Daddy barked, "I told you this was a mistake. She always gets car sick on this road. Too windy, I reckon." Daddy's voice sounded irritable, and I began to wonder if we were going to turn around and go home, something that had happened a few times before.

It was a sunny, sultry, summer Saturday in 1955, and I'd been promised a birthday lunch at the S&W Cafeteria in Knoxville, a spectacle like nothing I'd ever seen with fresh flowers in the front windows, mirrored walls, a winding, red-carpeted staircase with gleaming handrails leading to the mezzanine and another marble staircase cascading up to the second floor. Live organ music saturated every inch of the high-ceilinged, ornate dining rooms decorated with panels of acorns and oak leaves. Once inside, it was hard to take your eyes away from the magical wonderland filled with pungent smells, vibrant colors, and mellifluous sounds. The bustle, laughter, and constant stimulation of the senses were addictive. Everyone who entered seemed to become happier, energetic, and so alive.

The grand, art deco building with the enormous S&W sign out front had anchored the center of downtown Knoxville since 1937. Its revolving doors drew in smartly-dressed men for business lunches and elegant ladies who chatted while sipping tea in hats and gloves, and it was a hub for civic club meetings. There was a sign in the lobby that read, "Meet your friends here" and I was certain that meant me. I'd heard my mother say they served more than seven hundred people an hour for breakfast, lunch, and dinner every day and couldn't understand why we hadn't been there before. There was nothing like it in Newport.

I'd been there only once before and remember whining at the end of that lunch, "I want to live here for the rest of my life," as my father bolted out the doors into the street and declared that we would never be back because it was just too expensive. But here we were heading in that direction for a second time so that I could have a birthday lunch of lasagna, crisp lettuce and cucumber salad, and a large scoop of their famous homemade chocolate ice cream, the same things I had on my first trip and declared to eat on any subsequent trips that occurred due to an incessant amount of begging, hinting, promising to practice my piano exercises two extra hours each week, and an occasional short stint of crying.

The aromatic smell of their spicy lasagna and the taste of the homemade chocolate ice cream were fresh in my mind when our car had backed out of the driveway at ten that morning and they were still fresh in my mind but in a rather distasteful way as I tried, to no avail, to keep my eyes forward and my stomach from lurching.

"Oh-oh," I said putting my hand over my mouth just as I began to throw up all over the floor in front of me.

"Stop the car. She looks pale. I need to try to get her some water or juice from that house over yonder," Mother blurted out.

Everything became a blur. The air in the car was hot, I was hot, and I hated heat. I hated summer. The next thing I knew, Daddy had pulled over to the side of the road and Mother was out of the car walking through someone's yard and knocking on their front door, then disappeared inside for a few minutes.

Daddy said, "Get out of the car and stand next to it on the yard side while I check out something under the hood. Watch out for cars and don't get run over." So, I crawled out of the back seat just as Mother came out of the house with the woman who lived there. They were carrying some cloths, a bucket full of water, and a cold glass of orange juice. I drank some of the juice and Mother wiped off my dress and shoes while the lady cleaned out the floor of the back seat with her wet cloths.

Just about the time we got everything cleaned up, she got thanked, and I was feeling better, the lady said, "Lord, Lord, what's the matter with your car?"

We hadn't noticed the smoke coming from under the hood and water running all over the place from under the front tires. Daddy's head was still hidden by the uplifted hood, so we went around to see what he was staring at to find him holding up a piece of black hose that looked like it had melted.

I had learned early on not to pay too much attention to the arguments my parents had because it was a daily routine, but I suddenly remembered the one they'd had a couple of days before when he was dropping wrenches and banging around on things with his head under the hood of our little black Ford that always sat in the driveway next to the house. I listened through the open den window and remember her saying, "You know you have no idea how to do this and you should take it down to Mr. Parrot before we try to drive to Knoxville Saturday." His response was loud and matter-of-fact. A fellow at work had showed him how to do it and he knew exactly what he was doing, and she should mind her own business. That was followed by her quick exit into the house, the slamming of the screen door, and little conversation between the two of them until we left for Knoxville two days later.

"I don't think this car's gonna make it to Knoxville like this, do you?" the lady said to Daddy, who didn't respond right away. They continued to look at whatever there was to look at in silence, then with arms folded and leaning back in his usual defiant stance, he finally spoke without addressing anybody in particular. "Well, it looks like all the water's run out of the radiator, so I guess it's gonna heat up on us."

"Let me go inside and wake up JimBob. He's pretty good with cars, works on 'em over at Carlisle's in Jefferson City during the week and may be able to fix it so you can be on your way. You two come on in the house and get out of this hot sun. Ain't no use to stand around here waitin' for somethin' to happen. Them freckles 'll be twice that size by the time this gets fixed," she said, patting my head. Mother glared at Daddy, and we followed her into the house, leaving him by the car.

JimBob was a redheaded, bearded lump of a man about two heads taller than Daddy with arms that rivaled sides of beef. But he knew his way around cars and when he saw what had happened he went right to work, walked back and forth to his shed to get supplies, put together a temporary connection to fix the problem, and filled whatever had leaked with water.

An hour later, Mother and I were back at the car when JimBob slammed down the hood and said to Daddy," Now, if I's you, I'd take this straight to ole man Parrot up in Newport tomorrow. I don't think I'd drive it to Knoxville today 'cause this fix I put on it 'll only last about twenty miles and that'll get you back to town but probably not much further." Daddy mumbled something I couldn't quite understand and then tried to pay him, but he just walked off back toward his shed, dragging a long piece of hose, and carrying a huge wooden toolbox.

The lady said to me and my mother, "Y'all come back sometime. It was right nice talkin' to you. I had a feelin' we was related."

It turned out that she had been married to one of my mother's second cousins up on Cosby, but when he got accidentally run over by a revenuer who was chasing a moonshiner, she moved down to Reidtown and married JimBob. She said she met him at the gas station and married him the next week because she'd been looking for somebody that could keep her car running and he fit the bill.

She patted my head again, turned me around to make sure we got all the specks of vomit off my dress, and we got back into the car. She leaned against the door and sniffed in my direction, then said, "I done the best I could to get everything off that floor but if still smells tomorrow, I'd pour the bakin' soder and water to it by the gallon, if you know what I mean." Mother thanked her again as Daddy cranked up the car and we turned around toward Newport.

I never made it to the S&W that day, my parents didn't talk for about a week, and I got an extra piece of the leftover chocolate layer cake for dinner that night. It was several years later that I realized I had previewed what my life would be—a life without the fix-it gene.

My lack of talent to fix things appeared much later, about three years into marriage, when my mother-in-law decided that my husband and I needed a dog. We were no longer in graduate school, had jobs and a house, so in her mind, it was time to expand our family. To her, that meant animals. We had both grown up with dogs and I missed having one, but I quickly found out from my husband's groaning complaints at this prospect, that he had apparently merely tolerated them, had no desire to have another one, and dogs were nowhere on his radar. But this was a gift from his mother, and we decided it would not be prudent to decline it.

My mother-in-law's house had always been home to both cats and dogs (shelties, miniature poodles and other varieties) but she was currently infatuated with schipperkes—a small Belgian dog bred to catch rats on boats, looks much like a black fox without a tail, has pointed ears, sheds very little, and is crazy smart—and now had one of her own called Tony. I had become well-acquainted with him on visits to her house and was told that he tolerated very few people but oddly seemed to like me a lot. So, our visits always included walks with Tony, sitting with Tony's head on my lap, and long moments when Tony stared pensively into my eyes until I gestured for him to get up on the couch to get petted. We were sympatico. My mother-in-law commented on this frequently, so it was no surprise when she decided that I needed one of my own.

My husband had already declared that we couldn't have a dog in the house, and I was used to having outside dogs, as well. The new addition would sleep on the covered carport and be let into the house on occasion with supervision only. So, a suitable doghouse had to be found. It was decided that we would get one from a local hardware store, which on the surface seemed like a great idea since there was one that had several varieties set up to view in the pet zone of the store. We went there on a Saturday, looked them over carefully, picked out one that seemed the right size and bought it. We asked when it could be delivered since we couldn't get it to fit in our car, not having a truck. Happily, it could be delivered the following Monday and would be in place when the puppy arrived. Since both of us worked, they were instructed to leave it in the carport. Everything seemed perfect.

On Monday afternoon, we drove down the quiet, winding road toward the little red brick house we were renting, in anticipation of finding a large box that contained the doghouse. Instead, as we turned the last bend, we saw a rather long, rectangular box about ten inches deep, lying in the center of the carport.

"What's that? It can't be the doghouse. It's not the right shape. They must have delivered the wrong thing," I said, getting out of the car.

"Oh, no, don't tell me we have to put this thing together," grumbled my husband, beginning to examine the label. It was only then we realized we had never asked, and that particular information was never given. We had naively assumed it would magically appear on our carport, looking just like we saw it in the store. After a few minutes of stunned silence, we discussed whether to take it back or try to put it together. The latter seemed like the only option. Where could we get one already put together? We had no time to look for another one. Besides, how hard could it be to put a doghouse together?

After ripping open the box and pulling out the innards—including a table-size fold-out sheet of directions that listed everything in the box plus fifteen diagrammed steps to the process and tools required to complete the job—we were immediately stalled by a lack of suitable tools. We didn't own a hammer, screwdriver, or pliers. We'd never needed them before and hadn't anticipated needing them now. A quick call to a nearby hardware store, getting ready to close for the day, saved us from despair. The owner locked up as my husband left with his loot—plus a few extra items that "looked interesting"—secured in a new red toolbox. Not able to face any other challenges that afternoon, assembly would be delayed until the following day. That was when I found out that those who lack the fix-it gene unfortunately attract others who lack the fix-it-gene.

"No, it doesn't fit on that way," I said, turning the directions upside down, trying to figure out which side we were working on.

"Well, it's going to fit on that way now because we already have one on the other side and there's no place to put this piece except right here," he said emphatically, pounding the nail into the piece of wood that was slightly too long for its current location.

"It's a good inch and a half too long. We can't just leave it sticking out like that." My super-symmetrical neatnic brain waves cringed.

"We'll saw that part off once we get everything else finished. Obviously, they didn't put all the right parts in that package so forget about those ridiculous directions. I know where everything is supposed to go so let's just get this thing done," he said, picking up another long piece that looked like it should fit somewhere onto the back, but ended up on the side.

I dropped the directions in exasperation onto the carport floor and said, "I'll go to the hardware store. What kind of saw do we need?"

"How should I know? Something small, I guess. Tell the guy there what we're doing before you buy anything big enough to cut down a tree."

I returned about thirty minutes later with a small hand saw—bought from a scrawny little man whose closest relative must have been a wire-haired terrier—to find the doghouse had apparently been finished in my absence. It turned out that we had hit the jackpot. There were several unneeded items in the package that we could surely use for our next fix-it project—three slats of wood of various lengths, some strange looking pieces of rubber that were later discovered to be weather stripping, two clasps that seemed to fit nowhere, and a slew of extra nails, screws, and brackets. We sawed off the sticking-out part of the too-long plank into a jagged, chewed-looking edge and stood back to view the slightly sigogglin domicile that appeared quite uncomfortable on the uneven floor of the carport. No more was said about it and the leftover items from the package disappeared.

Little Jacque de Noirmont (who we subsequently called Jocko), AKC registered with all the papers, arrived at our house the following Saturday when my in-laws came to visit from Chattanooga. He was a three-month old puppy but had already been trained by my mother-in-law to do everything but cook dinner. She took one look at the doghouse and said, "Well, we need to spruce that up a little, don't we?"

By the time they left for home on Monday, the little carport shelter had a new rug inside and fresh paint on the outside walls, there were new bowls for water and food with instructions on when, what, and where to feed him, and an admonishment to always keep him in our sight because he was a purebred dog and somebody might want to steal him, which happened while we were at work exactly two months after he was permanently ensconced on the carport, where he was tethered with a light-weight, flexible, long chain that allowed him to wander around the carport and out into the side yard during the day. After several days of worry about his fate and certainly not telling my mother-in-law that he was gone, putting reward notices in the newspaper and posters around the neighborhood, I woke to the slamming of a car door in the front of the house and the squeal of tires as a familiar bark took over the early morning air. I threw on my robe and ran to the front door where Jocko greeted me with a whirling jump into my arms. He had been returned by someone who figured out what we already knew— that he had a mind of his own, hated everyone but me, would eat only salads of lettuce, cucumbers, and radishes, chewed on slices of limes for dessert, and was too ornery to risk waiting around for a reward.

It was a few years and two houses later before we tried out those tools again. Apparently, the pain of our first venture into the construction process had completely vanished from our psyches when one day my husband decided that we could easily put together a set of bookshelves for our home office. This required another trip to a hardware store; except this time, we knew the shelves would not arrive at our house ready to use. The following Saturday would be the day for assembling the shelves.

When I woke that morning, I discovered that my husband had read through the directions, discarded them, as usual, and surmised that the perfect place to erect this masterpiece was on the deck—which was about fifteen feet off the ground and attached to the back of the house—where we could enjoy the fresh spring air while we worked.

I rounded the corner of the house to find that all materials had been emptied from the box and laid out on the deck in no particular order. My job was to hold things (packets of screws and bolts, screw drivers, metal clamps, and pieces of the shelving) until ready to use. About fifteen minutes into the project, a doghouse flashed through my mind just as I heard him say, "You'd think these people would put the right stuff in these boxes. Here we are again with pieces that don't fit anywhere." He was holding two pieces of metal of different lengths and described how they should both go on the same side of the bookshelf, which was barely taking a recognizable shape. I offered to get the instructions but was informed that the directions would be no help since they had come from China and the Chinese don't construct things the way we do. Plus, we were so far into the assembly that it would be hard to figure out where to start in the outlined process. Instead, I was directed to put down the packets and hold up one side of the bookcase so that work could continue on the other side without the whole thing completely falling down.

As I was placing the packets on one of the deck chairs, several of the screws fell out of one that was open. As I grabbed for them, the side of the shelf I had been holding up fell on the chair and knocked the other packets off, causing several bolts to roll onto the deck. We had not considered that since the deck was made of long wooden planks, the screws and bolts might fall through to the ground below in places where the boards no longer fit together tightly. No cloth had been placed under the work area to prevent that. We stared over the edge of the deck and realized it was useless to try to find them in the thick grass.

The next few minutes were filled with expletives, orders, chaos, regrets, and a vow never to do this again—since we were obviously incompetent at anything having to do with assembly—as the remaining sections of the shelves were put together with some of the materials that were originally in the box plus random nails and screws found in an old cabinet drawer in the basement. Several odd-lengthed pieces (obviously meant for someone else's bookshelf) were tossed into the trash. The bookshelves never made their debut in the home office. They ended up leaning against the outside basement wall and languished there for five or six years—barely able to hold a few light objects without falling down—until they were sold for two dollars in a yard sale to a man overheard telling his son that he'd "take this mess apart" and make some bookshelves out of it.

The Blue Box

"Have you ever seen as many fat nurses in your life?" Mother barked in eyebrow raising, gravelly fry tones—her best get-your-attention voice.

Through cataractous lenses she spied me hurrying toward her, a forefinger raised to my pursed lips, shouting "Shh!" Did she not comprehend that they were within earshot and would remember her every disagreeable word the next time she pressed that call button for some necessity—navigating to the bathroom, taking medication, or getting physical therapy?

I mumbled my worries and picked up speed, whizzing by open doors that emitted searching faces onto the narrow hall. I pretended not to see them as a cacophony of ear-splitting buzzers and intercom voices cut through the air.

Parked in a wheelchair beside the nurse's station, Mother's head sat just below a withered potted plant's dying brown leaf trails, barely hanging on, reaching out to her right shoulder for comfort. Three nurses and a physician's assistant stood behind a long, dented and scarred, shoulder-height wooden barrier, eyes locked on mountains of paperwork. Everyone in the hallway had become deaf to her. She did not exist on their plane.

No heads turned as she cranked up the volume and repeated the derisive question with embellishment, ascending pitch, and stridence—ending fully in the coloratura soprano range—pitches I never knew she could reach. "Can't you hear me? I said, 'have you ever seen as many fat nurses in your life?' They might as well not be here. They never come when you call."

I didn't respond, just pursued my objective—diverting her attention as soon as possible.

Mother's insolent greeting was a shock the first time I heard it, but after two months it had become an ostinato accompanying every visit to the low-slung, redbrick, sixties-style building that sat on the far rise of a slightly uphill, pockmarked driveway, edged by straggly-limbed bushes and pieces of broken-off asphalt. The exterior revealed little of its contents except visitors' cars crammed into too narrow slots in the front parking lot—a perfect location for removing small bits of paint from the sides of already dinged car metal—and the sighting of an occasional incarcerated smoker let out by a side door for a breath of fresh air. When the outside keypunch door opened, each visitor was assaulted with an eye-watering, gagging smell that excreted from the innards of the nursing home where Mother was an unwilling guest at the beginning of her end.

Her new retreat was no more than a few hundred yards off the interstate exit. It was partially hidden behind a run-down used-car dealership filled with chop-shop specials and a popular, but dilapidated and cramped, meat-and-three café that left people waiting in the parking lot even on cold days, running their truck motors for lack of inside standing room or enough wobbly, scratched tables to sit down and eat. The restroom was outside the building and needed a key for access. So, even that was off limits to patrons until the portal had been accessed and the bill applied to the menu.

It was the only place to eat, other than a dicey truck stop and a bar, within several miles of the nursing home. Mostly, I avoided it, but had to resort to lunch there at least twice during mother's sentence and found that, on most days, if you could get inside just before the stated lunch hour of 11:00 a.m. it was possible to get served and out in less than twenty minutes. The faster, the better, since most items on the menu were either white and tasteless, fried hard enough for the locals to use as car blocks, or painted some shade of grey and swimming in grease. The corn bread, soup beans and turnip greens, being the only identifiable offerings with flavors that resembled their facade, were what I honed in on when there was no time to drive into town at lunchtime.

With each sojourn to mother's home away from home, my avoidance practice developed and was perfected. Before entering, I popped a mint onto my tongue to divert aromatic attention from disagreeable taste and smell sensations. After successfully entering the access code and passing through the small foyer, I would turn the corner, quickly maneuver past the front office—glass-concealed and filled with fake-greeting, dead-eyed, smirking management battle lines—and lurch down the long corridor, smile, engage dimples, and adjust my gaze to encompass the rows of abandoned, babbling wheelchair captives lined up against the wall, reaching out for familiar faces rarely seen. Then, I willed my body to become pencil thin so as not to touch anything that might remain on my person when eventually released from this dutiful, transitory imprisonment. It was a routine that I despised—but one that was required, since I was now the keeper of the blue box.

Temporarily funded by Medicare—a safety valve that would end within a few months—it was compulsory that Mother regain enough strength to graduate from this supposed full-care facility to an assisted living accommodation before the government money ran out. Currently, her status did not meet the assisted living requirements. She couldn't stand up without falling forward, refused to try to dress herself, and cried at the thought of having to leave, since the anxiety of change was more powerful in her mind than the anticipation of eventual comfort.

She needed help to do almost everything, or at least she seemed to think she did. I soon determined that the longer she stayed there the more dependent she became, now refusing even to brush her own hair. If she would have to remain in this eldercare version of prisons—found only in third-world countries—that would cost upward of $6,000 a month, I doubted she would last long enough for us to sell her house and everything in it to pay the bills, something that had already been brought up in confusing, hurried meetings with management that coughed up a phlegm of paperwork.

The assisted living option—a newer facility—promised parking spaces that didn't make visitors want to leave their cars on the side of the driveway, cost thousands of dollars less each month, advertised food tailored to healthy eating habits and had not discovered nerve-whacking buzzers nor intercoms. Unfortunately, it came with only one trained nurse on board and a requirement that clients—a term used to declare independence—be able to do most things for themselves. We would learn later that many of those enticing promises had deficits that were not advertised.

"Mother, please be careful what you say," I whispered into her ear. "They can hear you. Remember, your care depends upon their willingness to help you."

It had taken two weeks to get a phone in her room so that she didn't have to talk to me from the one at the nurse's station—something that was almost impossible to arrange—and remove the unexpected, agitated roommate who insisted on getting into Mother's bed and occasionally wearing her clothes.

There seemed to be no physical separation between the rooms or parts of the facility for patients who had senility and those who did not, except when demanded by family or caretakers. The danger of this was obvious to me and others who visited, but apparently not to the staff. Sometimes, disoriented souls walked in and out of other patients' rooms at all hours of the day and night without reason or notice; most appeared oblivious to any knowledge of where they were. Having no one checking on their whereabouts, they just sat down wherever their adventurous trek halted or climbed into any bed—whether empty or occupied—that crossed their path at journey's end. It didn't seem to matter. Hours could go by before a benumbed staff member noticed or chose to take action. Sometimes action was not taken until the person already occupying that bed began to scream in complaint or a visiting relative, shocked by the situation, scoured the building for assistance. It was amazing how often the halls were vacant of staff when some torment needed correcting. I worried about what would or would not happen once my car was speeding toward home, and she was left for days without an advocate until my return.

On a surprise visit during the middle of the week, a day when the staff thought I was several hundred miles away and none the wiser, I discovered that safety and care could not be guaranteed in this place without constant surveillance and advocacy of some kind. I had two days off from school and decided to drive there on a Thursday instead of my usual Friday. I didn't tell anyone, even Mother, that I was coming. What I found was surprising yet anticipated by intuition—unattended bedsores so severe that a doctor had to be called, clothes strewn about the room, dangerous medications given to keep her quiet, and the private bathroom so filthy that the local gas station would have been loath to advertise it.

From that moment, I assumed a polite but official voice when dealing with management and staff, one that Mother did not approve of, but became necessary in order to establish an overseer presence, to let them know they were being watched. Though artificial, it somehow provided a compartmentalization and sense of control for me from an out-of-control long-distance vantage point. No matter, I might as well have been circling the earth on an errant space capsule since my control was totally removed from reality. The controllers at NASA were more likely to listen to my complaints. Given that worry had become my companion, and absent caretaker, my moniker, a daily call to the facility and an occasional hiccup visit became my squeak in their wheel.

"Where have you been? You said you'd be here at 3:00?" It was Friday afternoon and TDOT never seemed to understand that Mother was waiting to release a new complaint when they planned their weekly interstate barricades that slowed me down. Six hours, two hundred- and twenty-five-miles separation and a later time zone didn't agree with either of us.

"Why did I let her talk me into leaving her in this boorish, inhospitable setting in East Tennessee instead of taking her to a nursing facility three miles from my house?"

This already-answered question kept flapping incessantly through the synapses every time a crisis occurred—a late-night phone call saying she had fallen out of bed—badly bruised but not broken—a blood sugar level of 425 that required the ER, a three-day delay in getting the doctor to call me back. The answer was obvious: a nagging guilt and anticipatory fear, but mostly an inability to be myself in her presence had clouded my thinking. I was again thirteen, an age I had not been able to escape in her mind's eye.

It had been a very ordinary morning that fall—a morning that did not yet include knowledge of the blue box—when the call, from a relative in East Tennessee, came to my office phone just before lunch. The day began at 9:00 and I was in my studio with a self-absorbed tenor who said he already knew everything about singing and made it clear at every lesson that he did not need a teacher, though he had to have the university credit, then at 10:00 the tall, off-pitch mezzo insisted on singing only songs about love—but they could not contain the word *kiss* since it was against her religion, followed at 11:00 by a soprano whose voice could cut through solid steel and showcased high notes that made my ceiling light fixture rattle. It was a normal day at the university, a happy day that invoked an uncanny enjoyment of teaching singers who required a delicate balance of tolerance, psychology, energy, and technical knowledge, though some days the latter proved to be the least important quality to possess. It suited me well.

That morning when our lives were fractured should not have come as a surprise, but it did. I had been expecting something like this for months, perhaps years, but avoided thinking about what would have to be done if it actually happened. Mother was on her own and I was too far away in space, time, and influence to affect change in the disintegrating environment that encompassed her daily life.

Worried because she hadn't called him about feeding the dogs, the man who took care of her farm out in the county had driven to town to check on her, then called 911 after he found her limp and unresponsive on the floor in the den, half under a coffee table, unable to move. She had been taken to the local hospital, the first hurdle in a marathon of obstacles to be overcome. Pneumonia and high blood pressure that only the Incredible Hulk could withstand sent her to hurdle two, a big hospital in Knoxville, where after two weeks of tests, ringing buzzers, doctors who came and went only when I was not in the room, and calling endlessly for too few nurses, it was announced by the social worker that she must be sent to a nursing home to recover since she could not pass the entrance test to their physical therapy wing. We were given three days to find one, a verdict dispensed with a smile and the names of several nursing homes in the area.

It had never occurred to me that finding a nursing home and understanding all of the rules attached to confinement there were more complex, time sensitive, and confusing than all hurdles passed when achieving my doctorate in music. Indeed, the latter was simple by contrast. It was sometime during this process that I became acquainted with the blue box. Once we were introduced, it became my constant companion and boasted several expandable divisions with colorful labels that defined various segments of Mother's life, the whole of which was now confined within its flexible shell.

"You bought the wrong kind of hay! You know I always feed the cattle that good alfalfa in square bails, not round ones," Mother said as I entered her TV-blaring room holding a vibrant, wildly blooming plant (no idea what kind it was) picked up on the way into town from the garden store just off the interstate exit. Her drab last-time-painted-in-the-early-'90s room needed a distraction. Several hours on the interstate had been long enough to dull my senses into believing that foliage of any kind could make a positive difference.

Trying to avoid the anticipated barrage, which I expected—knowing that she would eventually find out what she had now found out—I didn't respond, being surprised that she had found it out so quickly. I ignored her gaze, dumped my purse and jacket on the bed, set the blue box against the wall, smiled, and headed for the windowsill with the colorful reminder of someone else's life in the real world.

Just before the pot's base hit the metal plate along the bottom of the glass, she said, "Now, listen here. I called around and found out that you're changing everything down at the farm and I just won't have it. You'll be out of my will in a minute if I find out that you've sold any of my cows or calves. You'd better not even think about doing it."

"Now, there. That looks a lot better, don't you think?" I said in a strangely uncomfortable soprano range, trying to be upbeat.

"Does it have an odor? You know how allergic I am to smells," she responded with a frown. "I don't know why you bring plants in here. It'll be gone in a week. It'll either die from lack of water, get knocked off that ledge, or somebody'll steal it. Just take it back home. I don't want to have to worry about it."

Prior to the immediate circumstances, buying hay, going to the cattle market to sell cows and calves, or finding someone to bush hog the farm so that it looked lived on were things that had never even meandered through my brain. I was a town girl.

Both of my parents grew up on farms. My father inherited a farm from his aunt and when he died Mother took it over and kept it going. They visited that farm on a regular basis. But, during all of my growing-up years, they never gave me any usable information about how to keep a place like that going. I only went there a few times and rarely got out of the car. I developed a healthy fear of the cows and bulls, had no idea what to do with the goats—although I had tried some spectacular goat's milk cheese on a trip to England—and had never dreamed that one day I'd be the caretaker who worried if there would be enough rain in the fall or too much rain in the spring to provide hay for the cattle.

The Co-op had once been just a building that I drove by on the way to Jerry's fast-food joint. Now, I was on first-name basis with people there who sold feed for cattle—people Mother had done business with for years—and now they seemed to have a direct line of communication to her room.

Once Mother became ill, it was my lot to keep the farm running. There was no one else to do it. *Panic* is not a sufficient term for the mental state that suddenly inhabited my being. *Anxiety* seems too calm a word for the doubt, fear, dread, nervousness, and ignorance that took charge of all thought.

If Mother's man on the farm, a Godsend, had not been there to guide me along, *psychosis* might be the term to use for what would have become my state of mind. He told me right off that he'd been trying to get her to sell some of the cattle for years. Some were quite old, thin, barely could walk, and had been inherited from her father, then moved from his farm in another part of the county to hers.

"They're eatin' her out of house and home," he said, gesturing out toward the cattle standing in the barnyard. That fact became evident the first time I filed her taxes.

This was not a working farm to Mother. She thought of the animals as pets. So, when the cows had calves, she'd let them stay on the farm until they were too big to sell. She gave some of them names, apparently a no-no in the cattle business—like the one named "Baby" that had gotten out of the fence and been hit by a car on the road in front of the farm. It now lay, big and fat, down in the barnyard, having been hand fed for months, unable to get up and stand. Her hoarding instincts had taken over any sense of reality.

She'd been scolded by the local vet for letting it just lie there for almost a year.

"This is animal cruelty. That calf needs to be put down," he said, right before she fired him and hired another one from the next county over.

Since I didn't know Mother's farmhand well at that point, I did what I always do in uncertain situations; I sought a second opinion. In this case, it was from an old friend in town, a respected lawyer who also had a large farm with lots of cattle. He'd know what to do.

"You mean she's got forty-eight head of cattle on nine acres?" He closed his eyes, threw back his head, and burst out laughing, then gestured toward the heavens and leaned back in the swivel chair that wobbled right next to the window. It was a perfect place to see people pass by his office that sat no more than a block from the county courthouse. He had an air of "Southern lawyer" etched on every facet of his façade and persona.

When he was finally able to catch a breath, he sat forward, gestured across the desk, and drawled, "You've got to sell 'um off down to about nineteen. No wonder she's buying so much hay. They don't have enough grass to eat on that little bit of land. I'll bet she's feeding 'em that expensive alfalfa, too. Right?"

My confirmation sent him off into more gales of laughter followed by reminiscences of my mother and her eccentricities. He'd known her since he was a child, arriving at my house with his friends for Halloween parties, once dressed as Daniel Boone—complete with a real shotgun that my father was sure was loaded—and seeing her at every ballgame and school party until we all graduated high school. Since then, their paths had crossed often in this small town where everybody knew everybody's business but made darn sure they never mentioned it in public.

Thus, the cattle were siphoned off, little by little, taken to the livestock auction by the farmhand every few weeks until nineteen remained. I would drive over to the livestock market after each sale to pick up the check that would be deposited into her bank account. Mine was the only out-of-place car in a parking lot full of dusty or muddy trucks and trailers. After the first trip there, that brought stares due to my city clothes, I made a point to dress in barely-notice-you shirts and pants, no jewelry, and little makeup. After a while they got used to me, but the suspicion was palpable, since everybody there knew Mother, and nobody was used to seeing her sell so many cattle. It was bound to get back to her that her herd was being depleted.

Since an irrational belief that she might be able to return home had fueled her refusal to even consider going anywhere else including a new assisted living home close to her house, she was now frozen, afraid to leave this run-down, hometown nursing facility—one that required skills for negotiation and graduation. Unfortunately, neither was in sight on those weekly visits as I watched her body weaken, her hair thin, and her independence wane. Though still temperamentally combative, her staring, droopy eyes, slurred speech, and irrational discourse betrayed a lack of physical and mental stamina. If there really were rehabilitation sessions being scheduled to improve her mobility and strength— sessions that created bills—it was obvious that they had minimal positive effect. Somehow, she had to develop a considerable number of independence skills to qualify for relocation to that assisted living facility across town. Something had to change.

Could it be they didn't want her to leave? Elementary math and economics came to the forefront of my thinking. *They were about to lose a paying customer.* With dollar signs and the sight of a fading mother in my focus, I decided that smiles and pleasantries were not enough to get the attention of management and staff. Unless I moved quickly, she was going nowhere but down.

New attitude, new tactics: daily prodding of every member of the staff that could be located, a barrage of long-distance phone calls to the on-duty nurse at all hours of the day and night, followed by outright begging that employed all of my acting skills. I sounded pathetic and felt empowered. Within two weeks, things started to change. I had become a nuisance that must be eradicated. She was given much more attention. The nursing staff and rehab personnel started to call *me.* Her abilities improved considerably—she could now stand up and walk slowly with help and could maneuver her wheelchair, if needed.

With this new development, the assisted living administrator felt she could live there with minimal help, but Mother disagreed vehemently and worked hard to regress every time moving was mentioned. Everyone felt that it was her mental attitude that was holding her back.

She'd been visited several times by the management of the apocryphal assisted living, who dressed smartly and spoke of their facility in verbs and nouns that described vacation resort spas that Mother had never visited nor wished to visit. She was not impressed.

Mother became more agitated as the time drew near for a decision as to whether she would stay in the nursing home or move to the assisted living facility. She cried at the thought of leaving her friends, though none had names that she could recall. Some were wearing her clothes, and no one seemed to recognize her. The explanation of the huge difference in cost meant nothing to her. It was change that filled her mind with terror and brought on spells of disorientation. So, an excursion to this wonderland was arranged to allow her to see what release from confinement would bring.

One weekend, I went to see her a day early so that we could visit the villa on the hill just two blocks from her house, a fact that I began to mention more often since it brightened her mood and gave her hope that she would be closer to going back home. The assisted living management personnel arrived at the nursing home, put her in their van and off we went for a tour.

The view from the entrance over the surrounding area was lovely, there were flowers in the entryway, and everything smelled fresh and looked clean. It was stunningly quiet. There were no buzzers sounding, not even a distant telephone could be heard as we began our tour. We could hear and understand every word the assistant director said without asking for repeats, as had not been the case at Mother's current address.

She was shown the meeting room—she said she'd never liked meetings and had no reason to be in there; the activity room—she pointed out that she'd rather be on her own, didn't like crowds, and hated to play cards or sing songs with the piano; the dining room— she boasted that the food at the nursing home was as good as she used to get at the Coffee Pot downtown and doubted this place could come up to those standards.

"I hate to eat with people because I don't want anybody watching me while I eat. It makes me so nervous, I might choke," she complained after hearing that she would not be allowed to eat by herself in her room.

Finally, she was shown two private rooms. "This room is too dark. It only has one window," she whined, as we entered an empty room located in the middle of a hallway with a large window that overlooked a courtyard.

"It makes me feel claustrophobic. Why, there's no way I could get to the exit when this place catches on fire. I don't like this at all. I'm going back to the nursing home right now. It's a lot nicer, anyway."

All heads and eyes turned toward the door and her wheelchair was rolled quickly to a room at the end of the hall. This one had two large windows, one that looked out onto the front entrance and a side window with a grassy view.

"This one has a lot of natural light," I said, hoping for a better result. Its assets were pointed out. It was already set up with bedroom furniture, a small refrigerator and had a huge bathroom. She could move right in; just bring her TV, a lounge chair, and clothes.

"I hate being way down here at the end of the hall. Nobody will ever remember I'm down here. This is way too isolated. I'll have to keep the window open and yell out into the parking lot if I need help."

The following week produced nothing but vehement refusal to consider the new place as a possibility. Then, during the second week of daily phone calls, she seemed to slowly bend to the idea, giving me a glimmer of hope. But our last conversation before my weekly visit ended with, "I'm still not moving, no matter what you think. You might as well stay home this week. I'm not changing my mind."

I had given up all hope when I arrived that Friday afternoon at 3:00, walked into the room, and was greeted with, "I'm taking the corner room next to the fire exit. They'd better not have given that to somebody else. It has two big windows; one looks out on the front entrance. I'll be able to see people coming in and out of the building without getting out of my chair. I can talk to them right through the window if I want to and they won't have to come inside. Hurry up and call that woman with the bleached hair and make sure I can have it."

She had decided. Could it have been the casual reminders of the two-block distance from the new spa villa to her house, the discovery that one of her former neighbors was now a resident there, or the fact that my husband and I promised to put in a private garden for her to be viewed out the side window of her room? It didn't matter. She would be away from screaming people and buzzers; she could go to her regular doctor—not the always absent one that prescribed drugs over the phone without seeing the patients; I would no longer have to wear a gas mask on my visits, and the food actually resembled the items outlined on the daily menu. Freedom was in sight. Or was that just a delusion?

The blue box had become my obsession. It had to be within sight at all times. It travelled with me everywhere—an annoying, but vital companion, one that needed worrying about. It bulged with Mother's wallet and documents—a will, Power of Attorney, payment stubs, bank statements, electric bills, phone bills, insurance claims, Medicare statements, drug bills, Social Security receipts, Social Services information, correspondence from the nursing home—and numbers, important numbers—phone numbers, bank account numbers, social security numbers, insurance numbers, Medicare numbers, doctor's numbers, rehabilitation numbers—numbers that, if lost, meant chaos.

There developed a constant mental questioning about the location of the blue box.

Where is it? Is it safe? Is it still in the car or did I take it into the house or the motel or the nursing home or the wherever I was going?

Did I lock the car? Check it again before going to lunch or to dinner or to the drugstore or the grocery store. Can someone see it in the back seat of the car if I park on the street? What if it gets stolen? It should go into the trunk.

Should I leave it in the trunk of the car at the motel? What if the car gets stolen? Oh no! Go out and get it out of the car and bring it in and put it beside the bed.

Now that Mother was in the new assisted living facility, she was able to see her regular doctor, one that I had heard uncomplimentary things about from others in town. I had never met him and went with her to her first visit since leaving the nursing home.

"I thought you'd be dead by now with your blood pressure," huffed Mother's doctor—the one I'd been trying to get her to exchange for a real doctor the past few years—as he came waltzing through the door to face her parked against the far wall in her wheelchair.

"It's been a long time since I've seen you. You never have done anything I told you to do, so what can I not do for you this time?" Dr. Sarcastic whined in a monotone voice without really looking at her. Instead, while waiting for her to answer, he leaned against the doorframe and examined a large diamond studded ring on his left hand, as if it had just been placed there by some foreign monarch.

She stared at him through drug-glazed, blurry eyes and said feebly, "Well, why would you say that? I took the blood pressure medicine you prescribed and went through with the home health care, too. I haven't been here in a while because I've been in the nursing home, and they wouldn't let me see my own doctor."

She looked smaller than ever, frail, and pathetically vulnerable. Her toothless grin betrayed having not visited a dentist in more than forty years—apparently common practice for the area. I remembered telling my own dentist in Middle Tennessee that I was from a small town in the mountains near Gatlinburg and he remarked, "I'd hate to try to make a living as a dentist in East Tennessee. I've known several that nearly starved to death up there."

Dr. Sarcastic hadn't noticed that I was sitting just behind the open door on a little bench attached to the wall until Mother said, "We've been waiting in this cold room for more than half an hour. Didn't the nurse tell you we were here?"

Red-faced, he turned quickly toward me, almost knocking over the chair next to his examination table and sputtered something about having a sense of humor. I suspected the insensitive greeting to Mother had more to do with his most recent stay in a rehab unit, a noticeable dismissal of old people, and an itch to get rid of Mother quickly and find something to relieve his cravings than any sense of humor hovering over this colorless examination room.

He could picture my face printed next to the word "polite" in the dictionary as I said, "Now that Mother has moved to the assisted living, she'd like to be able to count on you to regulate her medications. We feel that she may be on some drugs that are not right for her, or the dosages may be incorrect since no doctor ever saw her at the nursing home and merely prescribed things over the phone," I said, trying to avoid Mother's glare.

Dr. Sarcastic opened her chart and scanned through several pages of notes sent from the assisted living facility while we sat in silence. There was an occasional grunt or a bob of the head as pages flipped. Finding something to his liking, he looked up, faked a smile, and pushed the thick folder to the back of the desktop.

"Well, I see that they've put you on a very potent tranquilizer," he said with a sound of gratitude in his voice. "That should keep you settled down for quite some time and happy as a lark."

This drug had been administered by the nursing home staff, as an antidote for anxiety—a condition that appeared endemic to that facility—during the fifth week of her incarceration. It was supposed to lower blood pressure and improve diabetes; the side effect being that one should feel calmer, at least that was what I was told. She was told nothing at all.

I had discovered this drug had been added to her regimen during a monthly scan of her drug bills—so many that the blue box's files could no longer accommodate them. When I noticed this drug—a very expensive one, one I'd never heard of, which I was paying for on a monthly basis—I questioned my own pharmacist about it.

Alarmed, she said, "Has your mother been diagnosed with bipolar disorder or schizophrenia?" When I said that I was certain she was nuts, but, "no" she had not been diagnosed with a mental illness, just high blood pressure and diabetes that were uncontrollable and seemed to be getting worse, she replied, "You've got to get her off that drug. It will make both of those things worse and turn her into a zombie; it may even make her psychotic."

That's when I had started my crusade to no avail. No one at the nursing home facility seemed to have the authority to stop the drug once it was prescribed. Since the original prescribing doctor was no longer working for the nursing home, the new, elusive doctor on staff would have to review the order and make a decision. But he or she, who knows which, never did. It was an impossible vicious circle with no end in sight for the duration of her stay.

Mother's increasing physical weakness and mental decline had become obvious to my husband and me. Now that she had been moved to the assisted living there was hope of making a change.

It was a year since her first dose of the new drug that we were having this conversation with Dr. Sarcastic, who also refused to take her off it until I handed him my Power of Attorney and suggested that we seek a second opinion from someone else on the staff at the clinic.

"Well, perhaps we could do a trial run without it and see how things go," he said.

Slash! It was removed from her prescription list. No gradual tapering off, no substitute drug in its place. Just stop and see what happens; not a plan generally recommended for getting off powerful psychiatric drugs like this one.

I now know that, apparently, there are persistent post withdrawal disorders, which occur after six weeks of drug withdrawal. According to research, they rarely disappear spontaneously and are sometime so severe and disabling that patients have to be returned to previous drug treatment. When their drug treatment is not restarted, these disorders may last several months to years. Recently, I was shocked to read that anxiety, disturbed mood, depression, mood swings, emotional liability, persistent insomnia, irritability, poor stress tolerance, impaired concentration, and impaired memory are the more frequent post withdrawal symptoms reported with sudden withdrawal from psychiatric drugs, which explains much of her behavior and general decline over the next two years making her life even more difficult as she lurched toward her end.

A few years after she died, I was passing by the TV one morning and was startled to see a commercial that gave contact information on how to join class action lawsuits against this drug manufacturer due to the fact that this drug caused high blood pressure and diabetes and was given to patients without those warnings, causing major injury and death. This news came a bit too late for Mother.

"What do you mean we never got along? We used to have fun. We did a lot of things together when you were little. Don't you remember?" questioned Mother, glaring up at me from her wheelchair parked in front of the small, under-the-counter frig in her assisted living apartment that never seemed to be tidy enough. What was that hefty monthly fee going for? Did anyone on the staff ever check on her, clean the room, or pay attention to her medical problems? My doubts were escalating.

Thinking hard about what she said, I tried desperately to remember a happier time with her as I straightened the bed, emptied the trashcan, and wiped down the sink in the bathroom. Nothing pleasant came to mind except her over-the-top delicious country cooking and the addictive chocolate cream pie she made every year for my birthday. I wondered if she really believed what she had just said. Then, looking in the mirror and noticing the obvious physical characteristics that didn't allow me to claim I had been switched at birth, I wondered if a few good memories could be obliterated by a multitude of bad ones.

My earliest memories are scant and foggy and weave around living out in the country with my great aunt in a house without running water or an indoor toilet. My father's parents occupied the house next door and there was room for a large garden in between. Each house sat on a good-sized piece of land and faced Route 411, the main highway from the mountains to Knoxville. Cars streamed by just a few yards from the front porch. Sometimes you could hear them all the way to the back of the house. With regularity, my aunt would part the lace curtains to look out the front window whenever an extra-loud engine brought her out of the kitchen, shake her head and say, "Them cars will be the ruination of young people. All they do these days is run up and down the road." I remember watching her throw up her hands, mumble something under her breath, and disappear into the kitchen again. She didn't have a car then and never learned how to drive.

Years later, when I was in college and home for the summer, my parents and I drove her down to Knoxville in their new Buick La Sabre because she wanted to shop at Miller's department store and take a ride on their escalator, something she had never seen. This would be her first and last trip to Knoxville, though it was only forty miles away. She spent the entire trip, there and back, rolling the back seat window up and down, jumping every time a car passed us, and huffing that it was a waste of money to buy such a fancy car with all kinds of gadgets on it.

The whole experience was a disaster. She was overwhelmed by the traffic, the department store's bright lights, the crowds of people, and a disappearing walkway that made no sense to her. After a few minutes of refusing to grab hold of the handrail or put her foot on one of the moving steps—with a line of people waiting behind her, she said, "Just take me home. This thing makes me dizzy." We left the store, went directly back to the car, and straight to her house without having lunch. Not what we had planned.

Apparently, my parents also lived in the house with my aunt in the first few years of their marriage. I have a few pictures of my mother standing on the front porch with me in the foreground. Oddly, I don't remember their presence in that house. What I do remember is running out into the back yard to look for my big hound dog after my aunt told me papaw shot her—the dog, not my aunt—because she got into the chicken coop. She was nowhere to be found and though I can vividly see every aspect of her face, including the white markings around her eyes and down the sides of her neck, I don't remember her name.

I remember finding an old, battered guitar—with three warped strings and one sticking out into mid-air—hidden under the couch and trying to figure out how to make it sound right. But I never could and there was nobody to teach me. Where it came from and who it had belonged to is a mystery.

A partial deck of Old Maids playing cards rummages through my brain from time to time. I can see myself holding them, looking at the colorful pictures on each one, and spreading them out in a circle while sitting on the planked floor in front of a worn, dark-colored couch with wooden arms, but I have no recollection of ever learning to play the game.

I remember watching Aunt Doshia (pronounced by everyone as Dosh) cook what she called "arsh" potatoes in the coals of the black, pot-bellied stove in the living room and wave off the "haints" every night before she went to bed, going from room to room swinging her broom through the air. As an extra barrier against them, she'd spit some of the snuff she dipped or the tobacco she chewed into a jar that sat against the wall by her bedroom door just in case one was still hidden in the shadows somewhere in the house.

Strangely, I don't remember where I slept in that house, where my parents slept, where I played, who I played with, or if I played at all. I just remember crying and asking to stay when my mother said we were moving across the street to a new house when I was almost four years old.

A couple of years later, my visits to Aunt Doshia grew fewer and farther apart when we moved several miles away into town. I remember missing her. Once when I was about eight or nine, I must have had a particularly bad day at home since it ended with a lot of crying and begging to go back there to live with Aunt Doshia. I don't remember what caused me to demand to move back to the country, but I do remember standing in the living room—after much pouting and red-faced begging—and defiantly saying, "Nobody loves me at this new house in town." My mother finally said I could go and packed a little pink travel bag for me with a change of clothes and a small doll we had bought at the Cherokee Indian Reservation store up in the Smokies. When my father came home from work late that afternoon, she told him what had happened and that he needed to drive me down to Aunt Doshia's. I remember the two of them going off into the kitchen to talk for a few minutes. When they came out, Mother said they'd come down to see me and bring the rest of my clothes when I got settled. But I remember starting to feel uneasy inside and when I got to the front door and out onto the porch, something changed my mind. I decided to stay. Was it a happy memory or a sad one that made me decide to stay? I don't remember.

"Are you listening to me? You've always been like your daddy. He never tells the truth or answers me when I ask him a question. There's no point in talking about it anymore," Mother said as she tried unsuccessfully to open the frig to get out her snack for the evening. She ate only one thing before bed, a small, one-serving Minute-Maid, pre-packaged orange juice and four peanut butter crackers that had to be made with Jiffy peanut butter without crunch and Keebler saltines with unsalted tops. No substitutions allowed.

"Wait, Mother, I'll do that for you. It's almost time for your show," I said, hoping to get her mind onto something routine and mundane.

Normally, when I was with her, I tried to avoid talking about anything except the weather, flowers, food, or TV shows like *Days of Our Lives, Jeopardy,* or *Wheel of Fortune,* which she watched religiously and had done since they began their run. I would try to extend these conversations as long as possible to avoid episodes like the current one that involved her negative perception of events or comments I had made in years past, most of which I never remembered. The ones I did remember generally had, for me, a decidedly different atmosphere in their intent than what she described.

This particular confrontation had come at the end of a niggly, accusatory argument, one in which I was reminded of several statements—ones that Mother swore she was repeating verbatim—I had supposedly made some twenty or thirty years before on subjects that I no longer recalled or cared about. On occasion, when this kind of thing happened, I did manage to recall the situation in question but remembered it as a time when I was attempting to divert her attention by being light-hearted, trying to make a joke or telling some story I had heard.

I'm not sure when it occurred, but somewhere around the age of twelve I was declared "mean" and met with a frown and a long harangue about a lack of respect for her opinion whenever I disagreed with her, so I developed a daily routine that involved little discourse with her on any subject unless I was asked a direct question. I don't believe it was a conscious plan but one that just evolved from a fear of saying the wrong thing, weariness at hearing the same accusatory speech over and over, and a need for self-preservation.

Several years later, I realized that my father had also developed this mode of interaction with Mother. This plan did not work well for either of us and ultimately created even more confrontation since quietude or introspection was also not permitted when Mother was present. Her need to know what you were thinking—especially if facial expressions appeared to have an inexplicable smile or smirk—caused her to pry mercilessly into your thoughts when faced with silence until answers—mostly false, made-up ones—were given or one of us left the room in a snit.

Unfortunately, in the years that followed, which involved the usual teenage hormone fluctuations, the ability to restrain my tongue did not last. Somehow, I developed a mind of my own and worst of all, a sense of humor, and it did not mesh with hers on most topics. She never initiated humor and I could never detect that she had any understanding of humor, except when she occasionally laughed at a joke told by George Burns or Bob Hope on some TV show she was watching. Even then, it was a rare event. When anyone in the house, family or guests, made a stab at humor, she acted as if every joke or pun—no matter the source or topic—was really about her and directed in some way to belittle some aspect of her character or personality. Her likely response to a story that should have elicited laughter was silence, a cold stare, a quick exit from the room, or a question such as, "What did you mean by that?" or "That didn't really happen, did it?"

To Mother there was only one opinion, one way to proceed on any matter, one way to do almost anything, and that was her way. All other options were scoffed at, not allowed, simply dismissed, or told to neighbors with a mocking, "You won't believe what she or he came up with yesterday," as if they were aberrations that needed reporting like bad news. On the one hand, Mother's need for complete control of everything that occurred within her house made life quite easy during my growing up years. I was never allowed to make my bed, wash a dish, or turn on the stove—though I often asked if I could help—since she was certain that I would not be doing it the right way. On the other hand, it meant that at age eighteen I arrived at college and didn't know how to iron or wash clothes. I had never made a pot of coffee or even scrambled an egg. There was much to learn.

I can no longer remember many things about my mother. My mind's eye tries to squint her out sometimes, but the grey cells' blurriness keeps specific characteristics hidden until some old, unearthed photo brings her back into the present. I see the shape of her body from behind, walking from the knotty pine paneled den between the long, narrow plastered walls down the hardwood floored hall to her kitchen. There was a time when Mother's face loomed in my mind at all hours of the day and night and my chest felt tight as if I couldn't breathe—right after some late-night, nagging phone call that ended with a random, derogatory remark about something terrible and embarrassing I had done in the sixth grade or while whizzing by cars on the interstate I would see her face, a phantom fixture in my rearview mirror. But now that she's been gone for twenty years, it's getting harder to remember the sharp sting of her voice, her pullback from a hug, her reluctance to say a thing was done well. I wonder if that is a good thing or a bad thing that I can no longer remember her as clearly.

She had been beautiful as a young woman. Her best friend called her "Miss Lake" after the ill-fated movie star of the 30s and 40s, Veronica Lake. Though mother's hair was not blonde like Lake's, it was a full-bodied, long, and wavy brunette and she had a presence that drew in the viewer. I still see that smiling young woman with dimples every morning in a family pictorial collage on my bedroom wall, standing outside her college dorm in a crisp white blouse and dark, flared skirt next to several flowering bushes. Who was she? What was she like back then? That person had disappeared by the time my memories of her begin. I didn't know that person at all. My memories of her don't include the smile, the joy, the sparkle in the eyes that come through in those early pictures. Something happened; perhaps many things happened to cause a once vibrant young girl to embrace suspicion, caution, and a fear of laughter as a way of life.

Given our dysfunctional history, whatever good times there might have been between us had been scorched by too many episodes of the opposite nature by the time she was trapped in this assisted living facility, dependent on me—a person she had never trusted to make the right decisions, the decisions she would like to make but no longer could accomplish—for keeping her affairs in order. Instead, she was simply waiting to die.

Mother didn't know we were cleaning out her house.

"Now, I don't want anything in that house touched. You just bring me the mail and leave the rest of it alone. Hear me?"
Mother said this each time I appeared for a visit on the weekend. I would nod and tell her the house was in perfect order, waiting for her return.

After two years of absence, it was obvious that Mother would not see the inside of her house again. So, little by little, items were removed from the house and taken to the dump or to Goodwill, sold, given to relatives, or transported to my house where some were put on display while others languished in large boxes in the basement, waiting for a permanent destination. There was no fear that Mother would know about this reorganization of her belongings since she had rejected the idea of bringing any items from home to her new location.

"There's no need to do that. I'll be back there before Christmas," she announced after the first three months in the nursing home, and after the first year at the assisted living, until the end of the second year when one afternoon of a very trying day, she greeted me with, "I'm never going home, am I?"

"I don't think so, Mother. I'm so sorry," I said, leaning in next to her, my arm around her frail body slumped into the captive wheelchair as tears made her cloudy eyes more red than usual.

"Promise me that you'll take care of the dogs til' they die," she said. I assured her that the two remaining dogs would be fed and watered every day as long as they lived and would get their Alpo sandwiches just the way she made them, though I knew they were now eating regular dogfood dished out by the man who took care of her farm. She and I, two strangers who had never communicated with any clarity of understanding, were not equipped to be comforters for each other in distressing times and never talked about what might be the end of her life.

Nothing was ever the same again for either of us. Over the next few weeks all energy and light gradually left her body. I watched her lose interest in anything she had ever desired to do. Even going down to her farm to see the dogs—her favorite pastime—became tedious, telling me to go ahead without her.

Late one afternoon during my weekly visit, she had a massive stroke while I was away from her room for dinner in Gatlinburg. She died three days later in a hospital in Knoxville, never regaining consciousness.

"I've always loved you. You can go on now, Mother. I promise to take care of the dogs," were my last words to her as she lay alone in a small, silent, stark hospital room that had only a single bed and one side chair, all life support having been removed, waiting for her final breath to expel. Her strong heart had held on much longer than the doctors predicted. My confirmation of a longtime promise must have been what she was waiting to hear. She died a short time later.

The blue box now sits in a downstairs storage room on the bottom shelf of a bookcase that holds remnants of memorabilia, important papers, and odds and ends. Though most of the accumulated clutter from her last three years of regret has been discarded, the blue box still holds clues to the evidence of her demise.

Clean Sweep

The grime-crusted concrete floor under the needing-painted ceiling of the covered back porch was indicative of the time that had lapsed since anyone living in the red-bricked ranch-style house had been able to see well enough, have energy of good health, or the desire to freshen up the place where I grew up.

It was once sparkling clean, stylish, everything in its place, with welcoming aromas of newly baked cakes and pies and pork chops or steak cooking slowly for hours in an electric skillet, corn bread baking in an iron skillet and fresh turnip greens turning into a savory delight filled with fatback and salt in a large pot on the back eye of the four-burner stove. Now, the odor of neglect had taken hold with a grip so tight that only a cataclysmic change could bring about renewal.

The tattered screen door was barely hanging on its hinges, no longer fitting the frame when we creaked it open, pushed the key into the old, rusty back door lock and entered the den that had once bustled with Halloween parties, Christmas get-togethers and high school bridge club meetings. Now, the stale, musty, cold air stung the nose and eyes as we closed the door, too overwhelmed by the enormity of our task to notice the mice scurrying into the hall closet or the silverfish later found hiding behind books on the den shelves or inside drawers. The room was barely lit, the overhead lights and table lamps covered in dust and grime.

It was mid-winter, a grey, overcast day, a chill in the air, no wind, just the sting of the cold on the face. The house had sat empty for months with only an occasional walk-through to pick up mail, check on windows and make sure everything was still there and free of scavengers or thieves. This was the first of many afternoons we would spend clearing out years of debris, memories, priceless objects, finding surprises at every turn until the house was bare to the walls and floor, leaving only the acrid smell of long forgotten quarrels, disappointments, and disasters in its wake. This process would go on for more than two years until time for the final purge. Mother would never see her house again.

Once inside the house, we whispered, tiptoed, and wondered why. The hardwood floors creaked as we moved through the den into the long hall connecting it to the rest of the house. The stillness was suffocating. Oxygen seemed to have been sucked from the premises. Doors and windows had rarely been opened since she left.

Mother didn't know we were dismantling her life. She warned us on almost every visit to her assisted living apartment not to throw away anything at the house. As we moved through the house, it felt as if she was guarding each doorway to make sure nothing moved out of the last mental picture she had before being taken away, terribly ill, weak and confused and unable to care for herself any longer. Due to failing health and a bad fall, she'd suffered through months of dislocation; first, in the hospital, then a nursing home, and finally an agreeable assisted living facility, while growing ever more irritable, disoriented, and distraught. The process of decline had taken two and a half years. With each visit, the gradual deterioration caused by diabetes and small strokes was obvious and irreversible. At the end, she was declining faster than I realized until one day, she simply gave in to death.

Dismantling a life is a messy, clotted affair, that in our case, required more investigation and subterfuge than organization. We already had the latter. Organization was our forte, but we had not considered that being a sleuth and expert at diversion would be much more useful in getting the job done. The process occurred in fits and hits and misses, and we discovered that full disclosure was not possible without eruptions of protestation from Mother until the very end, when disclosure did not matter.

The last trip before the auction company took control and finished the job was the first and only time we ever used a large rental truck for this process. The truck reservation had been for a much smaller one that would be easy to handle. But, when we arrived to pick it up in Morristown, twenty-five miles from Mother's house, only one size existed at the rental location. It was much too large for our purposes, but we had to take it since there wasn't a smaller size available within a hundred miles. After much growling around, wondering if we could get the big truck up her treacherous driveway, practicing reverse and gear shifts, we set off to Newport— my husband driving the truck that leaned slightly to the left, and belched, jerked and groaned at every gear shift—while I followed in our car. Once we arrived at her house, the truck was backed precariously up the sloping driveway, coughing, veering, and demanding to be let loose to race back down the hill. It took several tries to get it centered in the driveway, and unfortunately, on the first try it got too close to the house and dented the new gutters we'd had installed not more than a month before. Finally, it settled on the rise near the back porch where it was safely in place and ready for the haul that would be taken from inside the house on this late autumn afternoon.

We began the slow, intermittent process of clearing out Mother's house long before she died, before she expected to die, before she thought she would not return there, and before the day she asked, "Am I ever going home again?" when I had to say, "I don't think so." After that, we never spoke of the contents of the house again. We simply fell into a pattern during each visit. Sometimes, I drove the two hundred and fifty miles alone and sometimes my husband travelled with me. Either alone or together, we'd leave home early in the morning and arrive at her assisted living in midafternoon, park in the same spot under the shade trees in front of the newly-built one-story brick complex, walk through the well-kept and usually deserted lobby, look for someone to ask about how mother had been doing, but rarely find anyone, go down a short hall to her room that overlooked the parking lot and greet her with something that might brighten her day—perhaps a flower basket, a card, a story about a relative that would let her reminisce, or a bag of her favorite snacks. We'd talk awhile, go out to get her some supplies, return and talk awhile longer, then say, "We'll be back to visit once we get something to eat and check into the motel," before waving goodbye.

The next two days would be spent going back and forth from her apartment. There was errand running to be done. We'd drive out of town a few miles toward Knoxville to check in with the man who was taking care of her farm to see how the cattle were doing and take care of all farm business, take food to her two—there once had been fourteen—old, scraggly and lonely dogs that were stationed on a lot she bought across the road from her farm, tend to her banking business, pay farm bills at the Co-op and light bills at the electric company, buy supplies for her room and her fridge, visit with her off and on during the day, and take breaks for lunch and dinner. Sometimes, we'd put her in our car with her wheelchair in the trunk and take her to her favorite places to go until that final day when she no longer had the energy nor the inclination to leave her facility. Then, we'd go to her house and organize, pack up, throw away, give away, or load up the car with items to take back to our house hundreds of miles away, drop back by her assisted living for an hour or so, and then fall into bed at the motel around 9:00. That routine would usually comprise a three-day period before we had to make the five-and-a-half-hour drive home.

Over time, life dissolved into days, weeks, and months of waiting for the inevitable—the end that came as predicted years earlier, when her blood sugar and blood pressure were so high that the doctor remarked, "I don't understand how she is still alive. No one lives with a pressure of 360/150 and a sugar level of 400." That was five years prior to the end, when a massive stroke finally took her mind and her awareness, and her body began to shut down except for a fierce heart that beat on as if it could regenerate all other aspects of her bodily functions, until it couldn't.

Nothing that had entered the sprawling, brick house—added onto twice—had ever left. Nothing broken was ever discarded—no matter its condition. Several cabinet drawers in the pink bathroom—the one built in 1952—contained old, rusted, unusable toilet bowl floats, complete with their original arms and screws, that had been replaced years before. Each now lay carefully encased in its own brown paper bag, some rotting or eaten through by years of bugs crawling over them, as if waiting to be reunited with their original toilet in some afterlife.

Every dish, doll, scrap of paper, picture, book, check stub, piece of clothing, trophy, screw, gadget, and magazine was still there.

The house that was once beautifully habitable and impeccably clean had become a relic of years of dismay, distortion, sightless inattention to detail, and cobwebs of neglect plagued by overcrowded, superfluous, worn-down, and outdated items that no longer functioned or had a use. Now, they simply existed in living spaces, drawers, closets, hallways, bed tops, and counters, waiting for someone to give them a plan.

When I was growing up there, everything had its place and was not to be disturbed. Mother insisted that anything that was moved from a tabletop, counter, or bookshelf had to be replaced immediately to keep her equilibrium intact. Dusting every surface, every day was a necessity. No clothes could be left strewn across beds or chairs. They were always neatly hung or put away in drawers. Towels were stored by color and with neat edges. Beds were made with perfect corners and since no one could do it to her satisfaction, no one tried. Thus, when I went to college, it was the first time in my life I had ever made my bed and had to learn how to do it the right way from a roommate, who thought I must be an alien, having never made my bed nor washed clothes.

Somehow, and for reasons only she could fathom, Mother's old need for perfection had disappeared, revealing depression, disorganization, and disaster. Now, there was chaos where once there was precision. The dust on every surface was so thick that it clung to your nose and throat and brought on a cough and sore throat if in the house for more than a few minutes.

In her last few years in the house, Mother became a hoarder. She had long been a collector of antiques and a closeted packrat, not allowing things to be taken from the house that had once come into it, but never a hoarder. There was a definite difference between not wanting to get rid of memories and adding superfluous clutter to one's life. She had moved to the latter phase. It was as if she began to replace the people in her life who had died or left with things that she didn't need and would never use. Piles of new clothes, that she bought on sale racks at local stores and never wore, languished on her bed (tags still on them). The king-sized bed hadn't been slept in for several years, not since Daddy died. During his last few weeks of life, he had slept in the guestroom down the hall from their bedroom. He didn't die there, but she was certain that he had returned. She said that for several days after he died at the hospital down the street, she heard his ghost opening and closing the bathroom door that connected to the guestroom, so she moved permanently into the den at the other end of the house, afraid that he might come into her room while she slept. Their forty-seven years together had been enough.

Deciding what was trash and what was not trash occupied our initial dive into the jumble of envelopes with writing on the outside that said "important," drawers filled with old, random, crumbly papers, dozens of lists that related to the farm or to bank drafts or to nothing that could be determined, bags filled with unidentifiable items, wrappers, magazines, newspapers, rusted pieces of long-lost tools or parts from machines that no longer existed, and boxes of memorabilia from my schooldays and beyond that Mother had kept hidden away. Everything had to be touched, gone through, recalled for historical purposes, laughed about, pored over, and codified before being tossed in the trash or boxed to keep. There was so much. Most became part of the trash pile, but some were discovered to be quite important and needed preserving.

The walls throughout the house were in great need of paint and hadn't been touched in forty years. The curtains hung with lining in shreds, 1960s pillows, chairs, and couches—now back in style, but faded and worn from years of use or direct sunlight, and planting of body sweat—were brittle with dust and age. Closet doors wouldn't slide, stuck in place. Newspapers lay matted and stacked on stools in corners of bedrooms and halls. Piles of years-old antiques magazines and flyers from grocery store specials were so out-of-date that the stores no longer existed. There was a non-functioning recliner with a sunken seat, broken lift, and misshapen back. It had been in decline for years, but Mother refused to let go of it or let us replace it with a new one while she was still there.

The kitchen counters and drawers were overwhelmed with lopsided and dented pots, butter molds, utensils deformed by use, antique cookie jars, a toaster oven that had electrocuted anything crawling through it, a new can opener she had just acquired, and several faded towels and potholders with parts of mitts and fingers missing or burns that went straight through to bare threads. The kitchen stove was filled with ancient, sturdy iron skillets, handleless saucepans, and warped cookie sheets. She said things wouldn't taste the same with new ones. The refrigerator that hadn't worked well in years still contained jars of food that were molded over. It was all ready to be thrown out or auctioned! The new, never-used set of dishes we bought her ten years prior was placed neatly on one shelf, waiting for us to bring them home where they could feel part of an ongoing life.

Bedroom drawers were crammed with thousands of dollars designated as "money for the dogs," old tax records, bank receipts, and checkbooks dating to the 50s. Antiques large and small were everywhere in the house, so it was crucial to get the "good stuff" packed up to take home so it wouldn't be destroyed or stolen if the unoccupied house fell victim to intruders. One by one, each item was picked over, identified as "keep" or "auction," then wrapped well and boxed up to take home to sit in my basement until a determination could be made for their future.

Daddy had been dead twelve years on Mother's last day, but his clothes were still in the hall closet waiting to go to church or to work or nowhere and now to Good Will. Mother's clothes closet held a treasure of 1940s dresses and suits, shoes, and hats, all like new and hermetically sealed in hanging plastic bags. They would eventually go to a vintage shop in Nashville where they were devoured by the wide-eyed owner.

Mother seemed to have kept everything that traced my presence in the house. She had been a hairdresser in the early years of my childhood, as portrayed in years of class pictures that revealed all of the fad hairdos that she had practiced on me, while my body changed from short and very plump in the third grade to slim and tallest child in the fifth grade, never to grow another inch beyond 5'2." Stuffed closets held my music recital and beauty competition gowns, prom dresses, majorette uniforms complete with boots, batons, hats and capes, and my wedding dress. Stuck-shut drawers spilled out scrapbooks, report cards that said, "She talks too much," and a prize for the best handwriting in the third grade. The perfectly preserved sample was in beautiful cursive. Things had changed abruptly when my fourth-grade teacher said I held my pen incorrectly and insisted that I change immediately, making it impossible to ever return to that perfectly legible script. After that, writing was always a physical struggle, and no one, including myself, could ever read it easily again. Unmarked pictures of relatives she never mentioned, and her college friends, were impaled haphazardly into drawer crevices and falling out of scrapbooks. Since I didn't know them and had never met them, their visual presence brought immediate regrets for never having asked who they were and why she kept them so close without revealing their importance to her.

Mother had not had a Christmas tree in the house in more than fifteen years. Even then, it was a small, already decorated, artificial one that she would take out of the closet and set on the hearth in the living room each year when we went to visit. What we didn't know was that she continued to buy Christmas ornaments and other small artificial Christmas trees each year when they went on sale after Christmas. As we opened closet doors and under-bed boxes, we found enough Christmas ornaments to occupy most of the guest room that was now empty at the front of the house and would eventually become piles of Christmas items for auction, something the auction company thought was a win, win. The massive mound of glass, metal, and plastic that covered two-thirds of the room and reached more than five feet high in places was left to coalesce there until everything left in the house was auctioned.

Pieces of furniture were sold off as the house was cleaned out. As I finished itemizing the contents of the new Christmas room, I could hear Mother's voice as we backed down the steep driveway, making our exit from the annual Christmas visit over the past twenty years or so.

She'd wave goodbye and shout, "Next year we'll put up a big tree, so you plan to come a day or two early to help me put on the ornaments, OK?" As we drove away, we had no idea that new baubles would be added to her collection before we could get home. Though a big tree never appeared, it had apparently been mandatory for Mother to scour every after-Christmas sale to get the best price on what was left of the decorations, just in case one materialized in her living room.

In the years before Daddy's hands became gnarled with arthritis, he had taken an interest in refinishing a few pieces of antique furniture that still sat in the den, the hallways and the bedrooms, where they had been placed after being stripped to bring out the natural wood hiding beneath several layers of paint. One of the most beautiful was an old cherry wood secretary that had a curved glass fronted cabinet with four shelves on the left, and on the right side a mirror and fold-out desk, that when lowered, revealed six small drawers. Mother had displayed several pieces of her carnival glass collection on the shelves, but the drawers held old coins, artifacts from past decades, and items of great curiosity. One of the most curious was a small gun—the kind a well-dressed lady might have carried in her purse in 1900—that someone had given to Daddy. He may have said, but I no longer remembered how, when, or why it was acquired nor for what purpose. Our house had never contained a gun of any kind while I was living there nor in the many years after I left until he mentioned this one on a visit a few years before he died. He took it out of one of the small drawers and said, "This thing is so old it won't work and needs cleaning, I reckon. But, don't ever fool with it. Just leave it alone even though it's not loaded. It might blow up or something." I heeded his words. If Daddy had ever known anything about guns, it was news to me. He had been in the Navy in World War II, but he never mentioned ever shooting a gun before, during, or after that experience.

Now, we were cleaning out all of the insides of every piece of furniture and when we finally got to the secretary, there it was, that tiny gun still in its close hiding place, having been out of sight and out of mind for a very long time. I remembered Daddy's admonition and decided not to take it out of the drawer, just yet. We knew nothing about guns, were afraid to touch it, didn't want to be gun owners, and had no idea how to sell it. So, I called the man who took care of Mother's farm to ask if he would like it and he said, "yes." The next day he drove up to Mother's house to get it. When he took it gently out of the drawer, it was one of the few times I thought I saw him get excited about something. He cradled it in his hand with what looked like the beginning of a smile, turned it round and round, pointed it toward the ceiling, stared at it for a while and said, "It's got a bullet in it. How about that?" After he left, we fell onto the couch from relief that we hadn't pulled that trigger.

Mother's memory was intact almost to the end of her life and her inability to let go of anything, including the demand for refunds, had also remained solidly encased in the grooves of her brain. An old black rotary phone had sat atop a small oblong cabinet in the hallway to the living room since I was a child. It still remained when she spent her last day in the house. After finally determining that she would be going to an assisted living residence, we decided to cancel her telephone service since it was not being used and probably would never be used again. She was reluctant to do that and insisted we keep paying that bill for several more months until one day when we diverted her thinking and convinced her that it was wasted money she could use for other things such as hay for the farm, something dear to her heart. Since her phone was more than fifty years old, we assumed we would just throw it away. But, NO. She said it had to be returned to the South Central Bell office in Morristown where she would get a credit on her bill, an unexpected task that caused one to wonder what South Central Bell would do with that old phone. The task was completed with strange looks from all office personnel when we handed over the ancient phone and requested a refund, which we assumed we would not get and would never arrive even if agreed to. Our first mistake in thinking was that we had not accounted for the fact that this transaction was taking place in East Tennessee where all manners of business seemed to work on a different level than we had experienced at home. No questions were asked, the phone was taken from us, a receipt was dispensed showing that credit would be given and one month later it miraculously appeared on her phone bill when I received it in the mail. I then realized that I should have stayed in East Tennessee rather than move two hundred and fifty miles away where such a transaction would have taken hours on the phone, been transferred to at least four different people, some of whom spoke a foreign language, and eventually have my request denied and told that since the phone was fifty years old it would be better to sell it at an antique store.

The final clean-out days were filled with trip after trip to Good Will or hauling mounds of black bags of trash – dozens of it—to trash bins located near the train tracks downtown. One bedroom suit was sold to a neighbor, and another one to the kind and most capable woman who thoroughly cleaned the house from ceilings to baseboards for us over a four-day period. Two other bedroom suits and everything else that wasn't given away were auctioned.

I didn't go to the auction to see what became of the items that had been so carefully looked at before deciding their fate. I felt they should not be disturbed from their original position in Mother's mind or mine. New adventures and new dreams for each piece would take the place of those faded years.

Though we never told Mother anything about what we were doing, the increasingly distant look in her eyes at each successive visit revealed a resignation that her life was being dismantled piece by piece until it remained only in her memory.

Land Rover

The ominous-looking envelope marked *Urgent Notice* arrived at my house on a sunny afternoon in mid-summer. The return address was an important-sounding department in the State of Tennessee government. A state seal stared from the upper left hand corner of the flimsy-paper, odd-sized thin sheath.

Apparently, a warning signal embedded in my DNA causes panic in the brain cells when faced with any kind of official document that appears to have been birthed by some national, state, or local government entity. Do people ever get good news from those sources? Always assuming the answer is "no," something as benign as a jury notice has been known to cause stomach aches, shaky hands, and worry to the point of not being able to sleep for days. Unexpected correspondence from the IRS could put me in the hospital.

Normally, I take the mail out of the roadside box that leans slightly left—having been backed into by the man who delivers our wood for the winter—and walk back to the house before ever looking through it. Opening it while still on the driveway or attempting to read it in the glare of eye-squinting sunlight without my glasses on would never be an option. But this unexpected letter was on top of the stack, and it said *Urgent*. Not the kind of *Urgent* that is always stamped in blazing red on the outside of thick letters from obscure charities that pay their solicitors more than the intended poor children of third world countries receive from the donations that *must* be sent in before the impending deadline printed in bold across the back of the envelope.

This was quite different. There was no possibility of waiting until I reached the kitchen table to casually browse through the colorful flyers, birthday cards, invitations, sales pitches, and AARP magazine among the day's mail.

This particular *Urgent* meant urgent! So, I ripped it open, trying to hold all of the other pieces of mail under my left arm without dropping anything and read the greeting in bold: DEAR LANDOWNER.

I've never really wanted to be a landowner, except for the houses I've lived in. There have been only three of those and never more than one at a time. The idea of striding across a piece of land and looking out over vast acres from some hilltop—feeling satisfaction that a considerable amount of the planet we inhabit belongs to me—seems foreign. I had grown up in town—a city girl who rarely went out into the country except for an occasional visit with relatives—unlike my parents who were raised on farms and continued to keep some connection to the land, though they rarely talked about it and only in terms of the hard life they had while growing up on it.

I had avoided the acquisition of excess property until my mother became ill and died, leaving three properties to me in her will, a red brick ranch-style house in town—the house I grew up in—and two pieces of land out in the county. One was a large lot she bought to put her fourteen, stray, unvaccinated dogs on after neighbors in town complained about them barking too much and getting out of the fenced-in backyard at her house. Some of them were quite vicious and could be controlled only by Mother. Everyone was afraid of them, including me. They chased cars and people and caused chaos around the neighborhood so there was a collective sigh of relief when they were banished to the country lot. The other property was what remained of the farm my father inherited from his aunt many years before. Most of it had been sold soon after his death, but about ten acres remained when Mother died.

After Daddy died the farm became Mother's obsession, one that required time, worry, and money to keep it going. Her insatiable hoarding instinct didn't allow her to let go of anything ever brought to the farm, including newborn animals, which resulted in the remaining acreage being filled with too many cattle and goats until they had nothing left on the land to eat and barely enough room to roam. It was no longer sustainable in that condition.

The land now sat silent; the animals having been sold at auction once everything was handed over to me. But the land remained in my possession and still needed to be kept in good condition. Bushhogging and fence mending—now on my radar at regular intervals—were accomplished efficiently by the man who had been Mother's farm manager for several years. He was my only connection to the land and would call me to get approval for regular maintenance or if some disaster occurred that needed my immediate attention. Though I no longer had to drive the two hundred miles back home to get the work done and knew that he would miraculously fix whatever needed to be fixed, I hated to have to think about it and rarely did until the sound of his voice on the other end of the phone caused a tightness in my chest that grew to an uncomfortable anxiety level.

The lot and the farm were about a mile from each other and bordered what used to be the main road between Newport and Knoxville before the interstate was built. They were perfectly situated for development if and when the anticipated building of a new four-lane road from Sevierville would intersect with the old Knoxville highway less than a mile from Mother's land.

Mother had been predicting the highway's arrival for several years. She had admonished me on numerous occasions with, "Now don't you dare sell the farm and the lot when I die. They'll be worth a lot of money someday when that road comes through." I had seen no evidence it would ever happen and people who lived in the area were mostly skeptical.

At her death there was only one dog, Maxi—a gentle, shepherd mix with beautiful, laughing brown eyes, happy personality, and a thick coat—left on the lot and he was quite old, about ten or eleven. No one really knew. He was just another stray that had come to the house many years before and stayed to be petted lavishly and fed like a king. I promised Mother to keep that dog alive as long as I could and made sure that the farmhand went every day to feed him and give him water. I would visit Maxi and take him some of his favorite wieners when I was in the area, but that was only two or three times a year. It was a lonely life for a dog with no one to bring him Alpo sandwiches anymore, as Mother had done most of his life.

When Maxi had pals on the lot—other dogs in pens around him, Mother would go down to see them every day and bring their lunch. I can still see her with a long line of white bread slices laid out across the countertops in her kitchen, putting large globs of Alpo on the bottom slice then pressing the top slice down so that they were perfectly even around the edges. Then she'd stack them in groups of three, wrap them in foil, and put them all into a large brown paper grocery bag that would be placed neatly into the crowded back seat of her bird-stained, leaf-covered '86 Buick that hadn't been washed or properly cleaned out in years and sat in the driveway next to the back porch. Bits of old newspapers, rags used to dust off the dog pens, and bags of cat food filled all the spaces around the large empty square in the back seat designated for the daily dog feast. The car did have low mileage but had been eaten up by rats and squirrels that gnawed at the electrical system causing it to periodically refuse to start. Its most unique feature was the sagging roof upholstery, a problem she solved by using large safety pins to hold it in place. There were twelve at one count, but I suspect the number increased before she stopped driving it down to the farm.

When Mother became ill, there was no one to fix Alpo sandwiches anymore. But Maxi and three other scraggly dogs managed to live on with normal dry dog food for a couple of years. One by one they died and were buried on the lot near the old barn that sat at the back of the property. Maxi was the only one left when Mother died. He lived on alone for a year or so after Mother was gone but the last time I saw him I knew that he would soon just give up and die from a lonely heart. Not long after, the farm hand called to say he had been buried next to the others, the last living connection to my mother and her way of life.

Once Maxi was gone, I felt no need to keep that parcel of land but was still reluctant to get rid of it. What about the promised road that would bring millions of dollars? I would think about it later.

One day about two months after Maxi died my man on the farm, who was still looking after both properties, called to say that someone had dumped several trailers full of old tires on the lot and asked what I wanted to do about it. He said, "I don't have anybody to help me haul all of that off. My boys are off hunting and won't be back for a few days."

In a panic, I called a well-connected family friend in town—who happened to be a lawyer—for advice and gleaned that the culprit was likely one of his clients who lived in the area and was wanted for several infractions in the county, this being minor in comparison. My friend miraculously had everything removed almost overnight, I suspect by calling in favors and applying pressure in places where it was most useful and advantageous to those who committed the crime.

"If I 's you, I'd get rid of that lot 'cause this is just gonna happen again. You can't be an absentee landowner in this county and not have all kinds of problems," he said, in his usual Southern drawl. My next call was to the real estate agent who had sold Mother's house for me. He got the word out—probably to someone who knew about the road coming through—and the lot was gone in a couple of months. I felt considerably lighter, but there was still the farm to deal with on a daily basis.

I was still hanging on to the farm for fear Mother would appear over my bed in the middle of the night with her usual, "Now I told you not to sell that land. The guy you sold it to for nothing just sold it for a million dollars. You never did listen to a thing I say."

Though I had no glasses with me, I tried to read the letter from the state with blurry eyes as I walked slowly toward the front door. By the time I got inside and found my glasses, I was now certain that no good news ever comes from the government. It seemed that my land was in a county that was known for growing illegal marijuana by the ton—planes were flying over areas of the county's mountains daily and dropping markers where what looked like marijuana crops were hidden among corn fields, thick forested areas, or in small valleys between the hills. Once found, officers were dropped out of planes or drove there in all-terrain vehicles to chop it down. The Knoxville papers and TV news reports were full of these marijuana ambushes on an almost daily basis. Thus, according to this notice, I was now required by law to have someone walk the length and breadth of the land once a month and testify that there was no marijuana growing on it. If my inspector saw any marijuana, I was to notify the state immediately. If I did not and marijuana was eventually found there by the state flyovers, I would lose my land to the state and could be jailed or pay a considerable fine or both.

I decided immediately that ghosts didn't exist. I called my man on the farm and told him to start walking and report in. It took less than an hour after that call to decide it was time to call that real estate dealer one more time. Within days the farm was up for sale. My landowner days were going to be over as soon as I could unload this last need for meditation and anxiety control. I was ready to celebrate my freedom from recurring dreams of incarceration that included bad food, smelly cubicles, bells ringing at all hours of the day and night, and unflattering clothes that hung from my short frame, making me trip as I walked.

The real estate man worked his usual magic, though it took months of walking and reporting and making sure there was nothing fineable or jailable growing on those ten acres before it was finally sold for a price that I could live with. I signed the papers on a Friday afternoon and exhaled for the first time in months.

When I visit the mountains now, I usually drive by my old growing-up house and down to the country by the lot and the farm to see what has happened to them. The house no longer looks like I remember it. All of the big, shady trees are gone and a new driveway circles in front. The lot has trailers on it and the farm just sits silent, the old barn empty and slightly leaning from years of wind and wear.

On a recent trip there, I encountered several dump trucks and large pieces of equipment moving dirt in all directions about a mile before turning the curve toward my destination. It gave me an uneasy feeling. Just past the farm's entrance—with its old, rusted gate—I noticed the present owner had placed a For Sale sign on the front of the property in clear view from the highway. I stopped to visit two of the neighbors who speculated that the connector road from Sevierville would be finished in less than a year and that gas stations and markets would be all over that interchange soon. One said, "They're gonna be buying up property around here at prices nobody's ever seen. That woman that bought your old farm is gonna sell it for a bundle, I bet."

As I drove back toward the interstate, I began to worry that there really are ghosts.

Map Quest

"Hurry up and get in there before they all get off that bus," barked the voice of the scowling, gesticulating driver to my left who was past the time when protein would have intercepted his bark. Breakfast was a dim memory, having driven several hours through desolate, whizzing-by countryside on our carefully planned, much anticipated scenic drive west—a leisurely trip that was to take four weeks with a day or two to spare—and designed to connect us to every major city, landmark, historic monument, theme park, and national park west of the Mississippi while, along the way, visiting a couple of friends and relatives and eating at some fancy restaurants mentioned in Gourmet magazine. It was June 1980 and with this romantic getaway we were celebrating our thirteenth anniversary—upon reflection, a number that deserved more scrutiny.

A planner by nature, I like to know where I'm going to be almost every moment of every day. I start getting anxious if a vast void looms without any particular direction or time frame involved. My husband, normally similar in nature, though less confined by it, suddenly professed a need for adventure—a character trait that had never before surfaced since our first meeting in the early 60s. He was convinced that this trip should have a semi-rigid schedule with some destinations in stone, some more *ad lib*.

After beating down the "what if" squirrels in the back of my brain, I organized the trip to his satisfaction, made a few reservations here and there, and left room for spontaneity in-between. It seemed ideal when tracing the trip's course on the large foldup map of the United States—whose outline was now embedded in my mind's eye—that lay spread out across the kitchen table for several days as I agonized over our perfect jaunt across the country to the west coast, something I had never done and my husband had done only once; a trip he made with his parents and two siblings, during a mid-summer in the early 60s at a time when there were no interstates and the family car had no air conditioning. His most remarkable and often-told memories of that trip involved a cooler filled with dry ice that was wedged into the front seat of the car so that air from the outside vents blew across it miraculously simulating air conditioning in the more than 100 degree weather, constant complaining and fighting among the three trapped siblings in the back seat, the dire consequences of an unfortunate meal of spicy tamale pie at an uncle's house in California, and getting uncontrollable nose bleeds as the family reached the highest peaks of the Continental Divide—the latter being an omen that he would never be able to vacation in altitudes above 4,500 feet for the rest of his life.

Our trek was to lead south from Tennessee through Mississippi to New Orleans and west along the coast and southern border states with occasional sojourns that took us along the Cajun trail to hidden away places like the exotic spot where we found authentic boudin sausage in Louisiana or to the Texas hill country for what they claimed was "real western-style barbecue," then up the west coast to Oregon for a short stay where my husband planned to work with a famous conductor at a choral festival that he had been itching to attend. While he was busy there, I planned to bask in the predicted cool, crisp weather and poke into every nook and cranny of the quaint shops photographed in one of the inns magazines that I had on subscription. Surely the ash from the eruption of Mount St. Helens in nearby Washington State the month before would have dissipated by the time we arrived in Eugene.

Our return trip would drop us through Idaho, Colorado, Kansas, and a few states that required looking at a map to find and actually name, then back to Tennessee feeling rested, more connected to people we had not seen in quite a while, smarter—having seen places we had only read about in books—and much more in tune with each other, having shared a multitude of new, exciting and satisfying experiences.

Every evening we would get out the map, see how far we had gone that day, and plan the next day's escapade. I could see the car moving in my mind's eye across that map as we inched slowly toward the west. It would be a long trek and we had traversed only about four inches on the map so far, about a fifth of the journey.

"You must be really hungry. Didn't you bring a snack?" I said, trying for sympathy and knowing that Mr. Hyde only appeared when starvation was looming.

"My celery's in my ammo shorts and I'll get it out when we get parked," he growled, looking paler than normal. The shorts were packed in the hot trunk and the celery must be limp by now, I thought, but decided not to point that out.

Our car had suddenly come to a dead stop in the driving lane of a crowded parking lot that surrounded a fast-food place situated just off an interstate that sliced through Arizona. We'd been on the road a little more than a week and it was hot, very hot, hotter than usual for June—at least in Tennessee. It seemed to get hotter the farther west we drove. I thought of this every time we emerged from our air-conditioned cocoon into the drier than Tennessee, skin baking atmosphere that became more oven-like as we crossed the plains of Texas and beyond to New Mexico where the phrase "like a bat out of hell" became more real as we approached the opening to Carlsbad Caverns in 113 degree temperatures and were told by the guide that we'd have to wait a bit to see the bats fly out en masse. Waiting was not an option since anything above 80 degrees is hot to me. So, we ran for the car to press our faces against the air-conditioning vents while fleeing the dessert with Arizona in our sights. How odd that we had not anticipated this kind of heat.

When told about our plans and the length of time we'd be gone and out of touch with only a call to her every now and then—remember this was before cell phones—my mother had been skeptical about this trip, as she was about most things. She remarked that she'd worry the whole time we were gone but if we were determined to go all that way we had to see the Grand Canyon. Then she admonished us not to stand too close to the edge because we'd surely fall off and kill ourselves, followed by, "I'm just too nervous to have to come all the way out there and retrieve your bodies and your daddy can't drive that far with his arthritis." I told her that if we fell off someone from my husband's family would come get us, not to fret about it. I ended the discussion on what I thought was an upbeat note by saying that we would take plenty of pictures, which elicited, "Lord honey, we've got drawers of pictures that nobody ever looks at. Don't bother yourself on my account."

Unfortunately, we discovered that we are not really Grand Canyon people. Having driven hundreds of miles to get there, we walked from the parking lot onto a scary overlook, stared out across the vastness of it for a few minutes, took several pictures, remarked that it made us feel dizzy the closer we got to the edge, felt a little guilty that we didn't want to stay longer, and lurched into the beautiful wood and glass lodge nearby and ordered a table full of blueberry pancakes loaded down with maple syrup, sausage, eggs, and biscuits. Caloric intake was not a subject on my radar back then.

Now, with the Grand Canyon and a hearty breakfast a dim memory, the monstrous tour bus boasting a banner announcing SENIOR EXPRESS WEST was slowly groaning from the right of us into the parking lot of this oversized, orange-colored cholesterol heaven—the kind of place we normally avoided when given choices—miles from anywhere that looked like civilization. I hadn't noticed the impending doom until my husband repeated his command to disembark quickly, leaned across me, and pushed the car door open suggesting that I get out while he searched for a parking place. I was amazed he had such a long reach.

I jumped out of the car, bolted into the front door and had ordered by the time the first bedraggled, grumbling, slouch-hatted and wrinkle-shirted members of the senior bus hoard made it to the counter, the line stretching all around the inside of the restaurant and out the door. Whew! Made it just in time.

We ate at our usual pace. We sat down, then I got up to find extra napkins, went back to the counter for a straw and again for a fork, worked hard to get the mustard out of the slim bulletproof plastic packet, slowly unwrapped my burger and fries, removed the top bun to make sure everything that was supposed to be on it was actually on it, and methodically arranged everything neatly on the small table in preparation for my feast. Just as I took my first bite, George sat back down having taken his tray and the trash left over from his lunch to the bin in the far corner. He had wolfed down his food while I was still preparing to eat. His face now had color, his eyes were able to focus, and Mr. Hyde had returned to his dungeon.

Following lunch, we had just taken the turn to Scottsdale, Arizona, to go west to Nevada when our normally reliable car began to make death noises. We searched for a gas station with full service and more than one mechanic on duty—something only those over fifty remember—in the middle of town and found one almost immediately with a most agreeable attendant who diagnosed us as having a broken shock and in need of a new one before any trip farther west would be possible. He said it would be done in a couple of hours so having had no plans to spend any time in Scottsdale, we decided that this would be one of those spontaneous days to explore and also to call home to see how things were going with our house and dog sitter.

We found a phone booth and rang the home number, which was answered immediately by the friendly voice of one of my students who had agreed to water plants, check on the house, and feed the dog—a brainiac schipperke named Jacque de Noirmont (Jocko for short)—while we were gone. Jocko, who was AKC registered and came with papers to prove it, was given to us by George's mother, who raised schipperkes. He looked like a small black furry fox without a tail, could read minds, ate only salads and the leftover limes from George's gin and tonics, was perfectly trained by George's mother to obey all commands, never barked or bit anyone except tenors who tried to pet him, and seemed to like no one except this student and me. He tolerated George and they carried on a love/hate relationship until his death at fourteen—Jocko that is. His only problem had to do with a persistent skin irritation due to the intense heat in the summer that required an occasional cortisone shot. His genes came from Belgium where it was much colder than Tennessee.

Jocko was an accomplished traveler and normally went everywhere with us on short trips but this one was too long and complicated to take him. So, knowing that he would be happier at home than at the kennel where he shivered violently and stare-begged for mercy so intensely when we approached the place, even the vet suggested finding a home sitter for fear he would have a heart attack if we left him at the kennel.

"How are things going there?" I asked.

"Oh, things are great. The plants are wonderful, and all the roses are blooming like crazy. Are you two having a good time and where are you?" asked the student.

After filling her in on our adventures so far, I asked, "How are you and Jocko getting along?"

"Oh, he's a great dog. We go for walks around the neighborhood, and he stays right by my side the whole way without a leash. I fix his salad every day and he eats every bite then has half a lime for dessert. You should see the den right now," she added.

"Oh, really. What's different about it?" Starting to feel a little nervous at what might be coming.

"Well, you know how he scratches and scratches and I just couldn't stand to see him so miserable. So, I got this great idea. I greased him down all over with olive oil and I've covered all of the chairs and the couch in the den with sheets so that he won't get any of it on the furniture. He looks just like a little greased pig, and it seems to be working. He's quit scratching completely. I'll just keep doing this every other day until you get back in three weeks. Maybe he won't have to get those shots anymore."

I'm sure the silence was not as long as it seemed, but I couldn't think of an immediate answer. All I could do was picture a small black pig dog running through the house getting grease all over everything and sliding down the hardwood floors into the bedrooms at the end of the hallway while chewing on half a lime.

"Are you still there? I hope this is OK?" she asked, sounding a little anxious.

"Oh, sorry, I got distracted for a minute by a passing car. Sure, that's fine. Just be sure to close off the doors to the living room, kitchen, and the hallway to the bedrooms so he can't run around the house when you're not there," I sputtered, trying not to break into a laugh.

"Oh, yeah, I sure will, and I'll wash all the sheets before you get back, don't worry."

I said my thank yous and goodbyes and promised to call her again in a few days, wondering whether by the time I got home in three weeks he would either be cured, my house would have slid off the hill on which it was perched, or I should quickly buy stock in the olive oil business.

With new shocks and a full tank of gas, our car whizzed toward Nevada, a pass-through state that would take us to LA for a short visit with a friend I had met while studying in Austria the summer before. Each night the foldout map had taken its place on a motel bed or desktop to plot out the next day's adventures, but by now our car's travels were inching along slowly across my brain-map as we drove toward California. I didn't really need the physical one anymore to visualize where we were headed.

Neither of us had ever been in a casino, had no idea what a slot machine looked like, and the only kind of cards I had ever played with enthusiasm was bridge, a game not casino friendly and one that my husband hated. He dislikes card games of any kind and neither of us had ever held a pair of dice. Our sole frame of reference for gambling was my well-to-do uncle who was apparently born with the only gambling gene in my family. He travelled to Las Vegas on a regular basis and had won and lost buckets full of money, according to my mother. The relatives loved to tell a story about the time he won and lost more than a hundred thousand dollars in one weekend—with the word "lost" definitely coming in last. Not to be deterred, he flew back the next weekend and just kept playing until he won back most of what he had lost the weekend before. It was an addiction and a pattern that would continue for the rest of his life.

"Ok, here's your $2," said George after the car was parked in the casino lot with the blazing midday sun beating down in Reno. I looked at him in disbelief.

"What can you do with $2?" I asked.

"Well, we'll play the slot machines. We ought to be able to figure out how to do that. So, let's see if we can win up to $10 each," he said.

"Alright, but what if we lose the $2 right off?"

"Then we quit," he said emphatically. No gambling gene there.

It sounded reasonable to me. So, we lurched out of the extreme heat into the air-conditioned, glaring lights of the gaudiest place I had ever been. We stood at the entrance for a few minutes not really knowing which way to go or what to do but finally noticed the rows of slot machines.

"Let's play the quarter slots and see what happens," he said and sat down at one of the machines. I plopped down at the one on his right. We approached reading the instructions on the machine as if they contained directions for the assembly of a Mercedes-Benz. Finally, I got brave and put in my quarter and then another and then another and then another until finally the bells and whistles went off and I had won $5. Pretty soon $5 turned into $10. I had no idea it was going to be this easy.

George looked distressed as I kept ringing bells, and he kept losing quarters until he had none left.

"OK, let's take the $10 and call it quits," he said, getting up from his machine.

"This is too much fun and I'm feeling lucky. I think I'll play on for a few minutes," I said, sliding in the next quarter.

"You know you're going to lose it all eventually so you should stop now while you're ahead," he said, motioning for me to follow him toward the exit.

I barely heard his voice as I kept putting in the quarters until there was only one left. I dared not look up at him—now standing over me—as I put the last quarter in the slot knowing his face would have that "I told you so" expression. When I turned around he was already at the door and probably wondering if my uncle's gambling gene was lurking somewhere in my bones. Demoralized at losing such a big stake, we haven't been to a casino since.

We were right on schedule for rendezvous with friends and relatives in California when George stopped to make a phone call to someone back in Nashville. He was rather vague about it but said there might be an opportunity to write some kind of musical show. Given his background as a show writer for theme parks there was nothing much unusual about that.

"We should make it to the choral festival in Oregon right on time," I thought, as I waited for him to come back to the car from the phone booth outside a grocery store in Lake Tahoe.

It was an incredibly beautiful place filled with jeeps, rugged people who looked like Ralph Lauren ads, and a temperature that didn't require strapping bags of ice to your neck. We hadn't planned to stay there but I started wondering if we should spend a little time looking around. I got out the map and laid it across the hood of the car and plotted how we might take a couple of little detours to stay longer in this voluptuously forested area with lake and mountain vistas that could make two workaholics slow down for a bit, so different from where we had just been for much of the last few days.

As George strode back to the car I picked up the map, walked toward him, and started to point out some interesting side-trips when he said, "Well, it looks like this thing is going to happen."

"What?" I said, not really knowing what that meant.

"Well, they want me to write the main musical show for the World's Fair in Knoxville next year and we've got to pitch the concept for the show to the state in a couple of weeks."

"Wow, that's fantastic," I said.

"I've got to call them back when we get to Fresno to see when I need to meet with everybody, so we'd better get moving toward LA and not waste any time."

So much for Lake Tahoe.

We got in the car and headed west. At that point, the car in my brain-map was still inching along but I soon found out that the car in George's brain-map had just paid the entry fee for the Daytona 500.

About fifty miles from LA the sky in the distance started to look yellow, then brown, then like fireplace soot the closer we got to the city. I had never really seen smog in person, only on TV, so had no concept of what smog really looked or felt like until it began to close in on our car. It reminded me of an alien invasion movie I had seen at the walk-in in my hometown when I was about ten years old—a disaster movie where all the people were dissolved by a permeating cloud of alien dust that seeped into every pore and ate away at the body until there was nothing left but bones.

According to the local radio station, the city was under a high level smog alert, so we didn't want to get out of the car, much less stay there, and George surmised that since we were now on a somewhat faster schedule we should only have lunch with my Austrian friend and move on to Fresno where we were to spend a few days with family. Thus, other than a delightful lunch with a fellow singer, LA became a drive-through to Fresno. We saw none of it except massive lanes of parked cars baking in the hot sun as they crept along on the overcrowded interstates, brown sludgy-looking skylines, and glitzy people in expensive cars on a fast drive down Rodeo Drive in Beverly Hills, just to say we had been there.

By the time we got to Fresno, I was ready to park the car and chill out for a few days of catching up with some relatives who we hadn't seen in years, gape at the giant redwood forests and breathtaking waterfalls of Yosemite and relax without a need to move forward. Some of that actually happened but a planned four-day stay turned into two and a smidge with little relaxation involved due to a confluence of household oddities, a scenario that made visitors want to flee rather than lounge. First, we were shown the warning in writing on the outside of the frig that all items in the frig had a specific place and were labeled so and MUST not be moved, then the host handed each of us a towel and washcloth and stated that we were now holding the only towel we would receive for the duration of our visit even if we stayed a month, plus a mention that after three days fish and visitors begin to smell, all of which occurred within the first thirty minutes of arrival. Things went downhill from there over the next two days as we tried to appear invisible during bitter family arguments and unnecessary, excessive haranguing of the children. The oxygen in the atmosphere was getting thinner by the minute so that it was hard to breathe.

I could finally exhale when on the second full day George made another call—or so he said—to Nashville followed by a sudden announcement that we had to leave early due to an impending meeting about the World's Fair show. On a moment's notice our bags were packed—as if an evacuation notice had spewed from the local news—and we were out the door and headed east instead of north.

Apparently, we wouldn't be going to Oregon and the much-anticipated Bach festival after all. In George's mind, the original destination of the trip was now discarded and had paled compared to what lay ahead. After all, one could experience Bach anytime. George's brain-map car had already turned back toward home and was moving at breakneck speed.

Most of the upcoming reservations were cancelled as we sped through Idaho and slowed down briefly to wave our way through part of Yellowstone National Park. The only exception was Jackson Hole, Wyoming, where my brain-map car put on the emergency brake. It was a must-see. We had reservations at a historic hotel that was hard to book. I declared not to give it up and it was worth every bit of gravel the tires spun on to stay put for a day or so. We encountered more cowboy boots and hats, ornate silver belt buckles, and Indian jewelry than we'd ever seen before. The crisp weather and the spectacle of vast snowcapped mountains made our eyes fixate and glass over. It was hard to look away. I can still see the majestic Grand Tetons when I think of our drive over those steep, granite peaks as the car whizzed toward Colorado.

Now we were counting off miles per day in states covered rather than places seen. The brain-map car had become a Jetsons lookalike, skimming through little towns, along interstates, around big cities, seemingly never to touch the ground.

Blurrrrrrrrr!

Colorado was represented only by a one night's stay in Fort Collins where by accident we found an underground restaurant that was accessed by a futuristic glass elevator that opened into a speakeasy atmosphere filled with giddy people, the best food since California, and jazzy music that made the tart chardonnay go down smoothly. It was a jewel in the middle of nowhere with no above ground clue that these delights existed at all, just a small discreet restaurant sign that pointed to the elevator and then down.

We had friends who lived in Kansas but no time to stop to see them. They had told us that Kansas was flat but having never lived in a place that was actually flat we had no idea how flat, flat could be. Somewhere in the middle of Kansas we declared that we would never move to a place that was flat. The car wanted to go as fast as it could and got its only speeding ticket of the trip trying to escape the flatness. We drove for hours seeing nothing but flat until we finally approached Arkansas and began to feel like there was hope that something other than a level surface existed.

The foldout map had been put away long ago, interstate numbers were now embedded in our brains, and we silently watched our brain-map cars slide across Arkansas to Memphis where we expelled a sigh of relief that we were within one day of home. We had taken a little more than two weeks to get to the west coast and imprinted scads of details in our memories but lurched back to Tennessee in less than a week acquiring only a few lasting recollections.

This trip defined all vacations to come after. There would be no more road trips in cars that lasted more than two weeks and the words *vacations* and *visits to relatives* were never spoken in the same sentence again.

Air France

"Do you have any idea just how lucky you are?" asked my doctor, after peering for a few minutes at the four, angry-looking (once-red-now-mottled-orange-and-brown) stripes that stretched across the width of my back. They were equally spaced about four inches apart and coincided perfectly with the edges of the beautiful marble steps I had landed on in Aix-en-Provence, France, just ten days before when I fell down a flight of stairs in the middle of the night.

My husband, George, had been talking about going back to France for at least two years. Our four trips there during the 80s and 90s concentrated mostly on Paris and Lyon. We had never been to Provence. During those earlier trips, I was the planner, the navigator, spoke French when needed, and deciphered menus and signs because George's French was almost non-existent, having had none in college and no other reason to learn it since high school. So, very little vocabulary remained. Now retired from teaching, he had been enthusiastically taking a French class at the university for two years. His confidence was now bolstered enough to make him eager to get back to France and see if he could converse with the natives. His grandfather was said to be French—though that may have been apocryphal—and those genes may have prodded him back to his roots. Then, there was the exquisitely romantic Provence, with its vast fields of lavender, ancient ruins, and the markets filled with fresh produce, colorful textiles, and beautiful flowers waiting to be explored.

For some inexplicable reason, every time he brought up going back to France, I felt a sense of doom. It was an odd reaction that I couldn't explain to him or to myself. I just knew that I shouldn't go. It wasn't that I didn't want to go. I just knew that I shouldn't go. I had loved our other trips there—the delectable food, the incomparable Paris Opera, the impressive museums and historic churches that transported us to another place and time, and the boulevards that provided the imagination with unending stimulation as we sat under bright sidewalk cafe awnings sipping thé or café au lait and eating croissants while watching the fashionable and exotic glide by.

We had travelled a great deal in Europe over our forty-odd years together, but international travel has become so cumbersome in recent times that sadly, neither of us has really wanted to go back. So, this niggling desire of his that would eventually grow into reality was a surprise to me and one that I hoped would die from a lack of oxygen. Each time the subject surfaced, he sensed my lack of enthusiasm and would eventually drop it, grumble something under his breath, and wait until the next time it had to bubble up—perhaps a few months later—before bringing it up once again.

After a year of periodic nudging with no real positive response, a sense of urgency must have taken him over because one day a large picture book of France titled, *France from the Air,* appeared on the ottoman in our great room. The too-heavy-to-lift tome was filled with aerial views and descriptions of the most treasured, picturesque, and historic places in France, many we had never seen from any vantage point. It may have been on that ottoman for days or perhaps weeks without my notice until one particular afternoon when it was casually brought to my attention as we sat lounging during a conversation over drinks. He wanted to talk about our possible trip to France during the coming summer and excitedly showed me various places in the book that he had researched for exploration. It was all quite fascinating, the locales looked exotic, and we had the summer free with no particular plans. So, before I knew it, I had reluctantly agreed and once again began to plan an extended trip to France, though the sense of dread never left my chest as each puzzle piece was fitted together and the day approached for our departure.

I gathered all of my sources and planned hotels, restaurants, side-trips, rental cars, and flights. Since we were celebrating an anniversary, we splurged and stayed at one of the most celebrated and renowned hotels in Paris. Just off the foyer was a beautiful garden filled with exotic flowers and trees, a concierge who definitely hated Americans, and down a corridor their highly touted restaurant served such delicacies as an appetizer of six barely steamed asparagus with truffles. But it was Paris and according to my husband, we simply had to eat there because the food was acclaimed to be some of the best in the city. Unfortunately, its esteemed reputation did not materialize and after a meal of tasteless food that was overcooked, overpriced, and presented by a waiter who had been rejected from the Addams Family due to his sour demeanor, we wished we had found another option since the asparagus apparently cost more than a night at the hotel.

After three days of eating, sight-seeing, endless walking in the rain—due to never being able to get a taxi—and museum hopping in Paris we travelled to Aix-en-Provence by way of the bullet train that made passing trees look like pulsating camera shutters in old silent movies. On the three-hour trip we laughed, ate baguettes filled with ham and cheese, and drank sparkling water that we bought on the train. We talked about logistics—picking up our rental car and finding our intended destination, and the exotic and much recommended hotel, a lavish villa hideaway surrounded by lavender fields and cypress trees. One of our friends was wildly enthusiastic about her previous stay there and suggested that we use that as our point of exploration for the region. So, I had booked it for four nights.

The train arrived at the Aix station right on time. We noticed an angry dark cloud looming to the south—in the direction of our hotel—as we picked up our rental car, then began to make our way out of the airport—by way of several wrong turns—onto the main highway toward our hotel, which was located just outside the city center. We assessed that it should take about fifteen minutes from the airport, according to the map and directions given by the young man at the rental car outlet. But that was before the first sprinkles of rain hit the windshield, a French windshield that had controls only recognized by the French. After a good deal of button pushing and lever jerking, disclaimers of previous knowledge concerning how a car should work, and some shouting, the wipers suddenly came on just in time for the monsoon which was in full tilt and blocked almost any view of the highway or cars in front of us. The rain pounded so hard that the wipers were overwhelmed and though it was mid-afternoon, the sky was black as night. The next twenty minutes of terror on the highway were only superseded by the concern as to where we should get off since we couldn't see the exit signs until we were on top of them. Finally, I pointed to a sign that suddenly appeared out of the gloom, and said, "Turn here. We have to get off this road before we get run over."

The car lurched to the right and down the ramp toward the city and into the unknown. Having no idea where we were in relation to the map and original directions to the hotel, we drove around for several minutes, backtracking a few times—realizing that we were going around in circles—trying to find our compass. We asked for directions from people on three different corners and finally found our way to the small road that led up a hill toward our final destination. We stopped the car at the edge of the road, since there was no one behind us and sighed, hugged, and were relieved that we were nearly at our luxurious villa. We were almost there and couldn't believe our good luck.

George has always been a positive, hopeful, half-glass-full person who assumes that things will work out. Me, not so much. My what-if intuition kept nagging and the rain continued to pour as we slowly drove up the incline that led to the hotel and stopped in front of a call box with a prominent red button. There was a row of houses behind us and a huge, ornate gate at the top of the incline in front of us that was going to need to open in order to get to the Villa.

George rolled down the window and reached out into the pouring rain to push the button to let them know that we were there. A voice spurted through the intercom and after several crackling attempts to communicate, we discerned that we were to push the button again to open the gate and drive onto the property. That sounded quite easy. Oh, I forgot to mention that the rental car was a standard shift, a type that George had learned to drive during his teenage years and driven only a few times since, usually on trips to Europe where gear shifting was often a mystery. Thus, the real excitement began.

Perfect coordination is sometimes a difficult thing to achieve. In this case, it required that he push the button, then put on the brake, depress the clutch, start the car, and put it in first gear. But, when he tried that several times, unfortunately, he couldn't find first gear. Instead, it would slide into neutral and roll back down the hill.

The motor would die, and the car then rolled backward down the hill below the infamous box and button. As it was rolling, he tried to find first again, and it would slide into neutral and roll back even farther. He repeated this scenario with the same effect over and over. Each time he'd have to push the button, put on the brake, then depress the clutch, start the car again, and try to put it in first again, but never finding first gear, the car would roll back again. The gate would open slowly as we tried to get the car moving forward but just as the car started to roll backward, the gate would slowly close. He later realized it was going into third gear every time instead of first and he didn't have enough power to go up the hill.

After twenty minutes of this torture, I turned around and saw a tall, lanky, shirtless man leaning against his open doorframe just behind us, watching our ordeal. He casually smoked his cigarette, memorizing our every move in preparation for telling this bizarre story to his family later that day. Perhaps he had seen this before, perhaps he later exclaimed to his wife that there were more crazy Americans spewing money toward the exotic villa, or perhaps he was just bored, and this was a great way to spend an hour. He never moved, and his facial expression remained aloof as he watched us push the button, spin, back up, charge forward, roll back, wait, and try again.

This never-ending cycle sent George into such a depression that he began to weep. I was no help since I learned to drive on an automatic system and knew nothing about a standard shift. And it was still pouring! George decided to drive around the block to see if he could get used to the car and hope the rain would stop. So, we drove around for about fifteen minutes, parked for a bit, then came back to the dreaded hill and the box. The man was waiting for us in his doorway, apparently expecting our return.

Alas, our excursion around the block had not helped. So, another twenty minutes went by, continuing to run up the hill to the call box and press the button that opened the gate. Upon seeing the gate part, George would try to find first gear again, never succeeding and roll back down the hill as the gates closed. Finally, by happenstance and after about 30 more minutes, he finally found first, hit the button, the gates opened, and we drove through to the picturesque hotel, where we were greeted by the proprietor. After hearing of our dilemma, he said in perfect English with only a slight French accent, "You should have left the car at the bottom of the hill, and we would have retrieved it for you. It happens all the time." I realized that we were staring at him without speaking for at least thirty seconds. Did he try to tell us this over the muddled intercom or were we hearing this for the first time just now? It was hard to think.

"You are quite lucky," he said, walking ahead of us toward the door of our lodging, a two-level suite, that was outfitted with fabrics and furniture that looked too expensive to sit on or even touch. We had not asked for a suite but were "bumped up" at no extra cost to this one because someone cancelled. As I crossed the threshold, I was immediately gripped with that familiar feeling of dread and a coldness that fell over my entire body, though it was quite warm outside and only slightly less warm inside. I tried to shake it off.

There was a sumptuously decorated bedroom and sitting room downstairs and a huge marble bathroom on the second level connected to the downstairs by a winding marble staircase. It was a sight right out of *Town and Country*. We marveled at the beauty and comfort of each floor. Still, there was that dread in my chest that lasted right through dinner and into bed and "goodnight."

Somewhere around 3:00 a.m. I got up to go to the bathroom. As I was coming back down the stairs, holding to the railing with my left hand and being mindful to plant my feet securely on every marble step, it suddenly felt as if something either picked me up or just pushed me from behind. My feet and body flew up into the air and I fell on my back with a hard thud onto the marble steps. George had slept through it all, but then he had also slept through a tornado several years before. My yelling finally got him to wake up and rush over to help.

I could barely walk the next morning and the bruises were already quite apparent. So, I tried to walk slowly and be careful not to jerk anything out of place, but kept walking around, even several blocks to the center of Aix, to make sure everything worked properly. My only thought was that I really didn't want to go to a hospital in a foreign country and hoped that I was just bruised, nothing broken. His only thought was that we had to keep the ice packs coming and get out of this room and into one that had only one floor, which we accomplished before lunch that day. Now we were back in the ground floor room with the sunny windows and terrace we had originally requested. I wondered if the people who cancelled the suite had a premonition that someone was already in it and didn't want them to visit. As far as I could tell, they were correct.

"Yes, it's a miracle I didn't break something important, I guess," I said, trying not to squirm on the examination table while the doctor pressed and poked on various points of my back to make sure that everything was still in its original and intended location.

"It was such a shock when I fell with a boom coming down from the upstairs bathroom. I know it sounds weird, but it felt like something pushed me from behind and my feet just flew out from under me."

He frowned, picked up a form to schedule an x-ray of my spine, and said, "You seem to have the oddest accidents. After all, I do remember the camera falling on your head from three floors above you in the Chattanooga Aquarium. You were lucky that time, too. No concussion, just some profuse bleeding."

"Yes, I thought I'd been shot, the impact was so loud in my ears. You know the dent is still there," I said, automatically rubbing the spot near the back of my head on the left side.

He sat down in front of me while filling out the form. "And you weren't seen by anyone in France at the time? The pain must have been intense."

"Yes, it was excruciating for the first hour but got less so over the next few days. After George got me up and off the stairs, I just lay face down on the bed while he called the concierge and got a bucket full of ice to put on my back. The concierge asked if he should call a doctor. I probably should have gone to the hospital to get checked out, but you know how I hate doctors—sorry—and I figured if the pain started to subside, and I could walk then everything might be Ok. I just took some Tylenol and a sleeping pill and went back to sleep.

The next day we moved to a room where the bathroom was on the same floor as the bedroom. So, ice packs and Tylenol were my only medicine for the next six days."

"Well, I suspect you have bones of iron, and we'll find nothing but get this checked out and we'll go from there," he said, handing me the form.

Just as he was leaving the exam room, he turned and asked, "Wasn't there something about an old trunk you bought one time and had to take it back because you thought it was haunted after all the toilets in the house stopped working?"

I smiled and said, "Yes, I'm surprised you remember that."

"Hm, I think If I were you, I'd pay close attention to that intuition you have. It could pay off one day," he mumbled and went in to see the patient next door.

Fortunately, the scans showed that my back was intact, but my intuition was now on full alert and has been since that trip to France.

The Rehearsal Dinner

"Your husband certainly is fiery," whispered the slim, blond violinist in a low, sultry voice, leaning in to my left ear. The final word stretched into more audible space than any five-letter word would normally dare to occupy.

The musician's long, delicate fingers, flaunting perfectly manicured nails, lightly drummed the tabletop next to a white dinner plate—still bearing bits of an over-cooked and under-seasoned institutional meal, a fork and knife dangling precariously off its edge—as he stared directly across the table where George, the observed, was pressed between two animated middle-aged women like an anticipated PB and J sandwich being held by a five-year-old.

Stifling a laugh, I turned to the young man with sparking blue eyes, who appeared to be waiting for some reciprocal recognition of his admiration, and replied, "I agree wholeheartedly."

"Oh, shut up. Nobody wants to hear about that," barked the nasal, high-pitched voice of the bride's gesticulating grandfather seated at the head of the table. He could be heard easily over clanking utensils, gurgles of laughter, and undertone whispers coming from the eighteen guests wedged elbow to elbow around the rectangular banquet table. Oblivious to their conversations or occasional stares at his eruptions, the red-faced, balding octogenarian, who spoke only at a *forte* volume, had spent most of the evening purposely interrupting his son and two other relatives every time they attempted to make a toast, tell jokes, relate stories about the bride and groom, or do anything that might turn the attention of the captive audience toward their direction instead of his own.

Midway through the evening, when the conversation took an unfortunate veer into politics, he began yelling repeatedly at his nephew, "You're an idiot!" and, more than once, had to be restrained from rising out of his seat by the bride-to-be, the only one who appeared to be able to calm him down when his patience flagged.

The free-flowing wine had served to encourage the old man's outbursts, which became more frequent as the evening wore on, though the bride's mother periodically removed his glass to weaken the wine in it with a spritz of water when he wasn't looking. He seemed not to notice until the fifth or sixth toast. Suddenly, he brought his glass down from a full swallow, glared at his son and shouted, "If it's one thing I hate, it's cheap wine. Who picked this stuff out, anyway?" Denials filled the room. No one wanted to claim such a horrible decision.

Pandemonium continued until his attention could be diverted to blowing out a candle on top of the baked Alaska that had appeared from a side door and been placed in front of him by the bride. She once again saved the day by announcing that we were not only celebrating her wedding but the upcoming birthday of her grandfather. Laughter, applause and the singing of "Happy Birthday" diffused the wine debacle so that we could carry on as before toward the next inevitable cliff edge.

Sitting among the din, it seemed like eons since we were asked to take part in this wedding, though it had only been a few weeks. We had accepted what we thought, at the time, was a rather non-lethal invitation. After all, it was only a three-hour drive to her wedding location, and she was one of those graduate school friends that we had stayed in touch with and hated to say "no" to. According to the bride, our part in the celebration would be very short, but crucial to the mood of the ceremony. Each of us would read a selection from some of her favorite poems instead of singing—our usual wedding assignment—since her cousin, who was a violinist, would provide the only music. It was a relief not to have to rehearse with an organist or even warm up our voices.

The event would take very little time or preparation and be stress free. As a bonus, we were invited to the rehearsal dinner to be held the night before the wedding at what she described as the prestigious Faculty Club on the campus of the university where the groom was a respected faculty member. Having never been to the club but being aware of the somewhat exclusive, only-the-best-of-everything reputation of the university, we anticipated a gourmet meal with elegant service, and an evening of conversation with some delightful people—a very agreeable situation, indeed. Or so we thought.

We said, "Yes, of course. We'd love to be part of your special day." After all, she was a friend—not a close friend, but a friend, nonetheless—with whom we had performed, travelled, and even exchanged an occasional Christmas gift. But that was before the rehearsal dinner. It was before meeting the family of the bride and groom, who appeared to be people who held passports from several foreign countries that had nothing in common, did not speak the same language, and had apparently been at war for decades. It was before sitting for three hours in a stuffy, drab room decorated by a beige-obsessed designer—the walls, drapes, and carpet all just one tone of beige apart and topped by beige fuzzy-fabricated and fringed, shaded light fixtures and bright bulbs that the university must have retrieved from CIA surplus.

Following the wedding rehearsal in the chapel, George and I sauntered down the quiet, tree-shaded sidewalk lined with cars toward the imposing façade of the faculty club. Along the way we chatted with the Anglican minister who was to officiate the marriage ceremony. He had recently come to America from a post in England and was a svelte, distinguished-looking man in his forties with greying temples and smooth, tanned skin that lingered from his recent visit to Cancun. A much younger woman, who he introduced as a friend, accompanied him. She was tall, leggy and dressed in a cobalt blue, runway caliber wraparound silk dress that flowed elegantly as she walked. We had met them briefly at the rehearsal, where he expertly guided the wedding party through the ritual to be held the following day. The word "slick," in a sort of Mississippi gambler way, came into my mind as I watched him mingle after the rehearsal ended. His female friend sat in the back and watched the proceedings without interacting with anyone. She spoke very little as we walked to the reception and kept her hand on the minister's elbow right up to the front door, occasionally catching his gaze and flashing a secretive smile back at him, with lowered eyes.

Upon entering the large, marble floored and columned foyer hovered over by a hand-painted ceiling of flying birds, we were greeted by the bride, a natural blonde who looked beautiful in a flowing pink dress and silver shoes. Several members of the wedding party, who were not at the rehearsal, gathered around for introductions. Suddenly, a hand grabbed my shoulder from behind. I turned to face a bespectacled, heavyset woman with wild dyed-red hair and sparkling, over-large dangling earrings who grinned at the two of us, giggled hysterically as she threw up her hands and said, "You're the ones who got married at Lum's, aren't you?"

There was a definite silence. We looked at each other trying to figure out if she was kidding, out of her mind, or if the hovering birds had landed on her head and were devouring her brain. We began to talk at the same time—something we never did, sputtering out "no," "never did that," "why would you think that?" as many times as possible while she kept smiling and shaking her head "yes." Our protestations fell on deaf ears.

Of course, we had actually eaten at Lum's—famous for its hotdogs steamed in beer—a couple of times. But why would anyone think we got married there? It was a chain restaurant that we hadn't been to in years due to a major change in our diets. By the ninth or tenth denial, to which she continued to declare with certainty, "Now I know you're the ones, don't bother to deny it. I'm sure I didn't get that wrong." We finally stopped trying to dissuade her and just smiled in silence. She patted each of us on the cheek and said, "You two are just so cute," and waddled off, turning back to look at us with a wink. I hoped that would be the last of her for the evening, but it didn't work out that way.

We made it through the appetizers and were seated according to a plan divined by the bride's mother, who had spent considerable time and effort putting personality types together that would keep the evening cheery and pleasant, or so she announced as we entered the final destination for the meal. Now we were permanently ensconced in a seating design that could only have been created by an evil queen who loved to watch as her subjects squirmed.

Squinting up at the ceiling while rubbing her temples, the groom's aunt—yes, the very woman who was certain that we got married at Lum's and now sat on my right—put her hand on my arm and whined, "Don't they have dimmers on these lights? They're giving me an awful headache. Honey, do you have any aspirin or maybe something more potent?"

As it turned out, I did have aspirin and dug into my purse to find it. As I came up for air, I noticed that my spoon was no longer next to my plate where it had been just a minute before. Turning in her direction, I caught a glimpse of it as it slid from under the napkin on her lap into her purse. She was a master at diversion and by the time dessert was served, she had fingered and filed enough silverware and salt and pepper shakers from various spots on the table to outfit a party of her own on some future occasion. Her purse must have weighed fifteen pounds by the time she left the party. I suspect this was not her first attempt to magic away something she wanted to claim as her own. She was pro enough to work Vegas and never get caught.

Sitting on the other side of Aunt Klepto was the minister and his friend. They had been seated on the opposite side of the table, one person between them and George, for most of the evening but had moved to my side when dessert was served, exchanging seats with two of the groom's cousins who wanted to talk to another relative seated next to George.

Several times during the early part of the—lackluster-bland-wonder-what-that-is—meal, George had given me some strange looks—eyebrows raised and eyes and head slightly leaning to his left, which could have meant almost anything given the antics around us. I knew that look. I could tell he wanted me to notice something to his left, but I didn't know what it was until Mr. Slick and friend moved from George's side of the table into two chairs to my right. When they sat down, her wraparound dress fell open easily, showing off her long, tanned legs up to a point that was thankfully hidden by the draping tablecloth.

My attention was immediately drawn to them as they leaned into each other, whispered lips to ears, and ignored everything and everyone else in the room. They were obviously not just friends. It was made worse by George staring at me and then at them and giving me a look as if to say, "I told you so."

Not long after I saw my spoon disappear into Aunt Klepto's purse, my eyes were drawn to the tanned hand that was moving up the long legs of the wraparound friend. It was like trying not to look at a horrible wreck on the side of the road. You know you shouldn't look but look you must, for just a second, and when I looked, actually more was going on than I anticipated. I turned away quickly and wondered where I might find a concierge to order them a suite complete with room service, champagne, and mood lighting. However, apparently that was not necessary since they were so engrossed with each other that the present stark and chaotic accommodations and the CIA light bulbs only seemed to enhance the intensity of their mutual attraction.

My face must have given away the surprise because George's eyes opened wide, and his lips pressed together so hard that he had no lips anymore. I watched, almost about to burst, as he excused himself and left by the side door. I knew that I had to get out of there and as quickly as possible before completely breaking down. The violinist was talking with the person on his left and Aunt Klepto was at the prep table behind a large screen—I assume continuing to fill her purse with goodies—so I quickly got up and headed for the side door, unnoticed.

Once in the deserted hall, I could no longer hold the laugh I had been squeezing down. George was at the end of the corridor drinking water from the fountain and heard me. When our eyes met, we both started laughing so hard that tears were running down our faces. Desperate to get away from the other guests until this spasm passed, we opened one of the unlocked conference room doors off the hallway and went inside to laugh it out until we could calmly return to the melee and say our goodbyes.

A few minutes later, we set our pace for the banquet room door just as it was flung open by an exiting waiter and heard a voice from inside snarl, "Where the hell did my fork go? How am I supposed to eat this piece of cardboard without it?"

We hurried past the waiter on our way back to the conference room.

Is It Retirement or Abandonment?

"When are you going to retire?" I grew to hate this question over a period of more than twenty years. This was a question I started hearing in my middle fifties from friends, acquaintances, family members, strangers I met for the first time who heard how long I had been a teacher, and the president of the university where I had been a voice teacher for 30 years. I was not old. Why would I retire? Did I have something else I wanted to do? Did I hate my job? NO!!

What would I do if I retired? I had no hobbies, hate sitting around watching daytime TV, am intolerant of exercise, like to read but can't do it for more than an hour without getting tired and blurry eyes, need to be around people, and require a goal for the day to get out of bed each morning.

In my mid-fifties, when I looked in the mirror, I didn't look old. I was certain of it. At least I didn't look as old as some of my relatives did when they were in their fifties, and I was ten. No, I was not old by those standards. They looked tired, bored, unwell, and ready to retire. Many, including my father retired before they were sixty, sat on the front porch and watched cars go by, piddled around with their hobbies, or settled into a cozy chair in front of the TV in the den to watch their favorite soap operas.

I searched for the signs of old on a regular basis. How's my posture doing? Am I walking energetically, erectly, and carefully, and with no shuffling? Am I breathing deeply and giving enough space in the middle of my body to feel taller than my five feet two inches? All of this was important for a singer and especially important for an aging singer. So, I paid attention and taught my students to do the same. I was NOT old.

My hairdresser told me when I was thirty never to let my hair go grey because it was going to be ugly—emphasis on ugly—since I have freckles and red hair. She was right! I did not inherit my mother's beautiful, white hair with the natural wave. She had a different skin tone than mine, no freckles, and looked wonderful with her natural grey. When I started turning grey, I didn't really look older. Instead, when I stood in front of the mirror my father's face and baby fine, mousy hair—as he was at 57—stared back at me. This was not a look that was good on me. I looked like a vat of sewer water had been dumped onto my head indicating I should carry a sign that said "Contaminated, stay back." So, I covered up the greys with packages of hair dye that turned my natural reddish brown mixed with yellowish greys back to a color closer to the one I had when I was 35. I made sure that my posture was erect and kept my walking motion agile with practice and mindfulness.

My brain did not believe that I was old and had no idea that retirement was something one should start thinking about at that age or any age, for that matter. But, apparently, other people had some magic number of years allowed to be employed and I was not in on the secret. As time passed, parts of my body often felt as if they were hanging on to the skeleton with scotch tape and losing their grip, but my brain still assumed I was 35.

I worked every day to keep my body at the level it was when I was 40 or maybe better. Callanetics, tai chi, and walking would do the trick. I was certain of it. Yes, there were times when I was sick with a bad cold, a stomach virus, or a dead thyroid that needed medication, but I was not old!

As the birthdays moved on to sixty, then 70, and someone learned that I was still teaching, the exclamation became, "I thought you had retired!" A reason seemed to be required that would explain how blood was still flowing through my veins, my brain was still functioning, I was still enthusiastic about teaching, and students were still singing their hearts out in my office on a daily basis. So, it was necessary to let them know immediately that both of my voice teachers had taught until they were 92.

I was not old!

When the eye doctor said I needed new glasses to be able to see and my right eye couldn't be corrected, I was not old. Though my right ankle began to be stiff and required daily exercises to be flexible or when I limped and screamed with pain when I walked, I WAS NOT OLD!!!!

When I retired from teaching after 52 years to write mystery novels, I still didn't feel old until my optometrist, dentist, dental hygienist, gynecologist, vocologist, dermatologist, pharmacist, massage therapist, and ophthalmologist all retired within a year of one another. Now, I have to train a whole group of people to keep me going so that I won't feel old!

About the Author

Sharon Mabry is the author of *The Postmaster's Daughter* (Thorncraft Publishing, 2022), a mystery novel set in East Tennessee, and the humorous, memoir story collection, *The Blue Box and Memories that Live in the Bones* (2024).

Prior to creative writing, Mabry, who is an award-winning mezzo-soprano soloist and recording artist, premiered works by more than forty composers and made nine critically acclaimed recordings. She was a featured writer for the NATS *Journal of Singing*. Her book reviews and featured articles on women composers have appeared in several major music journals. She is the author of two books about music, *Exploring Twentieth-Century Vocal Music* (Oxford University Press, 2002, 2009) and *The Performing Life: A Singer's Guide to Survival* (Scarecrow Press, Rowman and Littlefield, 2012).

Mabry holds the Bachelor of Music degree from Florida State University, the Master of Music and Doctor of Musical Arts degrees from George Peabody College/Vanderbilt University, and a performance certificate from the prestigious Franz-Schubert-Institut in Austria.

In addition to her concert career, Mabry established a long tenure as professor of music at Austin Peay State University, where she received the university's highest award for creativity (the Richard M. Hawkins Award) and for teaching (the Distinguished Professor Award).

Sharon Mabry is an East Tennessee native, having grown up in Newport, Tennessee. She currently lives in Clarksville, TN.

For information about authors, books, upcoming reading events, new titles, and more, visit thorncraftpublishing.com

Printed in the USA
CPSIA information can be obtained
at www.ICGtesting.com
CBHW070043310124
3895CB00015B/1145